HOW TO SING A LOVE SONG

How to Sing a Love Song

*Loving Your Mate with Passion,
Intimacy, and Commitment*

Eugene Whitney

VINE
BOOKS

Servant Publications
Ann Arbor, Michigan

Vine Books is an imprint of Servant Publications especially designed to serve evangelical Christians.

All Scripture quotations, unless indicated, are taken from the *Holy Bible, New International Version®*. © 1973, 1978, 1984 by International Bible Society. Used by permission of Zondervan Publishing House. All rights reserved.

The names and characterizations in this book drawn from the author's counseling and personal experience are rendered pseudonymously and as fictional composites. Any similarity between the names and characterizations of these individuals and real people is unintended and purely coincidental.

Published by Servant Publications
P.O. Box 8617
Ann Arbor, Michigan 48107

Cover design by Eric Walljasper

95 96 97 98 99 10 9 8 7 6 5 4 3 2 1

Printed in the United States of America
ISBN 0-89283-931-7

Library of Congress Cataloging-in-Publication Data

Whitney, Eugene
How to sing a love song : loving your mate with passion, intimacy, and commitment / Eugene Whitney.
   p. cm.
Includes bibliographical references.
ISBN 0-89283-931-7
1. Marriage. 2. Marriage—Religious aspects—Christianity. 3. Intimacy (Psychology) I. Title.
HQ734.W575 1995
646.7'8—dc20
                                        95-24230
                                               CIP

Contents

Dedicated to my wife, Arleen,
whose life is a love song to me.

Acknowledgments

Appreciation is gratefully extended
to my friends and colleagues,
Rev. James Hale, Dr. Harold Sala,
Dr. John Hayden, Dr. Jay Martin,
and Dr. Arleen Whitney
for their professional manuscript critiques,
and
to Beth Feia, editor
and
to my parents, Lorin and Aimee Whitney
for their supportive love song.

Introduction

There are many kinds of love songs and many different ways to sing them. This book concerns itself with the kind of love song that is lived out in a marital relationship. What does it mean to sing *our* love song? It is *how we live our love toward our mate with concern for his or her well-being.*

In 1988, Yale psychologist Robert Sternberg wrote *The Triangle of Love,* a book based upon his research on love. In the book he proposes that the three essential dimensions to a loving relationship are *passion, intimacy,* and *commitment.* I am indebted to Dr. Sternberg for this conclusion, and have sought to organize my Christian beliefs about marriage around these three dimensions.

Passion is the first love song to be discussed. Too often marriages die for lack of passion. One reason for this is the misguided belief that we should only act the way we feel. Section I shows how we can keep passion alive in our marriage and restore it even when it is no longer felt.

Intimacy is the second major love song we can sing to our mate. I seek to show in Section II why autonomy is essential to lasting intimacy. Then I proceed to consider the two basic features of intimacy: self-disclosure and acceptance.

The third dimension of loving involves singing the love song of *commitment.* In Section III, I will show how we can strengthen our marital commitment by what we choose to believe about love, marriage, and God.

When we understand how to be passionate, intimate, and committed, we will have the basis for a love song around which we can arrange our own unique form of loving expression. Talented singers each perform in a unique way. Likewise, even though God has told us all the same thing—to love one another—we are nevertheless given a great deal of latitude to be ourselves and love our mate by singing our personally unique love song.

I have chosen to retain the traditional pronoun in references to God, although I am aware that God is Spirit, neither male nor female. It is not intended to be offensive to female readers.

Most of the names of people in this book have been changed to preserve confidentiality. Circumstances represent a composite of actual events, unless otherwise stated.

Although this book is purposely slanted toward marriage, the principles are applicable in any relationship.

Whether you are about to marry or have been married for many years, it is my sincerest hope that this book will speak to your heart and help you find confidence in singing your love song to your beloved.

Eugene L. Whitney, Ph.D.
Laguna Niguel, California

SECTION I

The Love Song of Passion

CHAPTER ONE

The Living
Love Song

Paula looks sad as she slumps into a chair in my office and puts her hands over her face so she won't have to look at her worried husband sitting next to her. Her drooping shoulders and her long blonde hair, hanging in disarray, speak volumes about her mood.

"I feel so bad," she begins. "I just don't think I love Randy anymore. I would like to do something about it but I don't know how to change my feelings."

Randy's eyes are red and moist as he struggles to make sense of what he is hearing. "I thought everything was okay between us... until recently," he says. "I still don't understand what's wrong."

Before me on my note pad are the symptoms of an ailing marriage: Randy is under enormous pressures at work to meet deadlines and hold onto his job. Paula is gaining weight. He is spending more time with their children than with her. He forgets to kiss her goodbye on his way to work. They haven't made love in weeks. At a time in their lives when Randy needs to pay special attention to romance, he is taking his desperate partner for granted. The more they focus on their problems the more their desire for each other fades. Love songs are forgotten. Moonlit nights are ignored. Dinners out are unscheduled to save money and time. Leisurely walks in the park are lost memories in the hurried press of life.

The young woman Randy married did not want to hurt his feelings; the young man Paula married did not want to burden her with his troubles at work. As a result, he was shutting her out of his personal life and she was preoccupied with his neglect. Both had lost all passion in their marriage because passion needs hope to survive and neither was hearing any strains of it from the other. They did not yet know about the living love song.

PASSION IS ACTION

Feelings of passion benefit a marriage because they are powerful motivators for us to act in loving ways. This passionate feeling of the desire for closeness is important in marriage because it fosters intimacy which leads to more loving actions.

Passion is both feeling and action. Feelings, however, change easily. They are not stable. It is normal for all of our feelings to fluctuate, and this is true for feelings of passion as well. Since fluctuations can occur from moment to moment it is not wise to base our love simply on how we feel.

Paula had felt excited when Randy was courting her. She had learned to associate her love for Randy with the romantic feelings he seemed to give her in those early days. "That's how love works," Paula had concluded. She assumed that passionate feelings would emerge whenever Randy would say and do the right things to make her happy. Without realizing it, she had taken a passive position, making her husband responsible to pump up her desire for him. She wanted to *feel* her love first so that it would be easy to *live* it. This was easier for her than acting passionately, which would eventually develop passionate feelings within her. However, passively waiting for our mate to "light our fire" is not sufficient to keep passion alive.

It is not reasonable to require our mate to inspire our feelings of desire. It is our own responsibility to keep our passion alive.

When it comes naturally, we can enjoy it! When it doesn't, we can do something about it even though we may not feel like it. By acting passionately, we can start to feel our passion return. Our love song starts to come alive. Sometimes we have to sing a few bars before we get into a singing mood. But by taking responsibility for being passionate, we can sing the first stanza of our living love song. *This is the love song that accepts responsibility for acting lovingly toward one's mate regardless of how we feel.*

Randy had fallen into the "squirrel cage syndrome": longer hours of work to make more money to support his wife resulting in separation for longer hours…. In his frantic race Randy became oblivious to the needs of his wife for more personal attention. He was providing economically but not emotionally. Paula was losing hope that her life with Randy would ever improve.

Hope is the fuel of passion. To survive, marital passion needs a reasonable hope for achieving closeness. If we ever lose hope of attaining that closeness, our passionate love song will lose its melody. But even hope is a matter of faith. "Easy hope" is always being able to see the light at the end of the tunnel. "Hard hope" is holding fast to our dreams and expectations even when we see no light at the end of the tunnel.

The stronger our hope, the more capable we will be of maintaining our passion. Our own inner attitude will have a direct effect on how passionately we love, even when we aren't in the mood to sing a living love song.

Passion cannot survive merely on unexpressed hope. Genuine hope should *say something*. Unexpressed desire seldom finds fulfillment, whereas expressed passion usually evokes a response. Not every response is satisfying, but if we do not express ourselves, no response is even possible.

Paula had not taken responsibility for her own passion, but had quietly waited for Randy to notice her. Had she insisted that they spend more time together, praised him for what he was trying to do, and become more assertive about her own needs for affection, she might have saved herself a lot of pain and trouble.

PASSION IS SEXUAL BUT...

Passion is usually equated with sexual activity. Certainly marital passion is likely to lead to sexual enjoyment. But passion is broader than sex alone. Marital passion is the desire to be close to our mate. When Randy and Paula stopped sharing their feelings with each other they no longer felt close. They tried to use sex as a means of drawing closer but it didn't work. Why? Because there was *no expression of passion in their communication apart from sex.*

There are people who have active sex lives with little else going on in their marriage. They use multiple methods for enhancing their sexual excitement. But the end result leaves them unsatisfied and trying harder. They are too focused on sex instead of upon loving each other.

Paula expected more affection because she and Randy had experienced more in the past. Before the pressures of financial survival hit them so hard, Randy had more time for them to enjoy each other. She never expected things to be any different and it was difficult for her not to take it very personally. When they did try to make love, Randy was too tired to enjoy it and Paula felt distant.

It is normal to hope that sex will make us feel closer to our mate, but sex alone cannot provide what we seek—the deep and lasting satisfaction of true closeness. Emotional intimacy can be satisfying without sex but sexual passion is not ultimately satisfying without emotional intimacy.

It is important to cultivate emotional passion before we try to fulfill physical passion. The ultimate fulfillment of passion is consummated through sexual expression, but it begins with emotional closeness. The husband and wife who know about verbal intimacy, self-disclosure, risk-taking, and sharing feelings with each other will approach sex as a celebration of the closeness that they have already achieved with their hearts. Love-making then becomes a satisfying expression of intimacy already established rather than a desperate attempt to fill a personal void.

DESIRE CAN BE DANGEROUS

All passion is not positive. Passion is energy that can be used for good or ill. Expressing our passion without good judgment is like letting an automobile engine control a car with no one at the steering wheel. There is a lot of power in an engine, but its constructive use needs to be under control. Similarly, feelings can be a powerful motivator, but their expression needs to be under the control of objective thinking.

I know a man who is passionately jealous and possessive. He lacks confidence in himself and is afraid his wife might leave him. She was originally very devoted to her husband, but his oppressive control and unrealistic demands are driving her away. His desire is destructive. It lacks objective judgment and self-control. To be positive, a passionate love song must be under the influence of constructive and loving principles.

NEW TESTAMENT LOVE

In the New Testament, the Greek word *agape* is used when Jesus tells us to love one another. It's used again when Paul tells husbands to love their wives. Scholars explain that this Greek word refers to the *will*, not to feelings. It conveys the idea of showing love by the way we act. When we love our mate with *agape* love, we are helpful rather than possessive.

The Bible clearly refers to love as a behavior more than as a feeling. In 1 Corinthians 13, the great "love chapter," the apostle Paul used behavioral terms and verbs of action. "Love is patient, love is kind" (v. 4), he said. "[It] rejoices with the truth. It always protects, always trusts, always hopes, always perseveres" (v. 6-7). The only time Paul uses feeling words in reference to love is when he is talking about what love is *not*. Love is not envious, proud, or easily angered. In 1 John 3:18 the apostle John writes, "Let us... love... with actions."

Feelings of "love" that are not translated into behavior are worthless. Feelings themselves are not love. Feelings come and go. They are unstable, unreliable. If we act loving only when we feel like it, our love will not be consistent.

The Bible teaches that how we treat others is the yardstick to measure our love, not how warmly we feel toward them. To obey the Scriptures and act lovingly toward a mate (or other people as well) is to anticipate that loving feelings will follow. Of course loving feelings make loving behavior more enjoyable. But even when feelings of love aren't present, we can act loving anyway. Eventually the feelings we are demonstrating will come along.

This is exactly how it worked out for Randy and Paula. She didn't want a divorce but she had lost hope. She was willing to try anything to feel her passion for Randy again, once she knew what to do.

She began by talking more openly to Randy about her needs, about her pain of feeling isolated. She took a risk and got his attention. His attention then gave her confidence to further risk finding out how he would treat her if she continued to act loving toward him. She didn't blame him or focus on past events that he could never change.

"Randy," she said one day following the counseling session, "I know you are tired, but we need some things from the market so I can finish dinner. Would you go with me so we can be together a little longer?"

"Well, I am tired," her husband replied. "But we haven't really seen much of each other lately, have we?"

She was happy that his response was positive, even though she certainly hadn't been eager to take the risk.

RESISTANCE

Too many sad and sorrowing adults wait for love's feelings to wash over them before they are willing to act lovingly. It feels phony somehow to act loving if our mate has just torn all our self-esteem to shreds with harsh accusations. Two important issues need to be addressed at this point:

First, the Bible never invites believers to put on a happy face if someone is putting them down. Jesus didn't drive out the money-changers from the temple with a grin on his face. Neither does God expect us to cover our pain with a smile that contradicts our feelings. But just because we might feel more like withdrawing doesn't mean that is the best response. We sing our love song by acting with care and respect while also sharing our feelings of hurt with our mate.

Sometimes our feelings of hurt are due to our own oversensitivity. When we are not getting our needs met in general, we are especially vulnerable when a specific need is treated as unimportant. We need to learn how to be more resourceful in meeting our own emotional needs so that we will be less sensitive in reacting to the needs of our mates when they hurt us.

Second, people resist doing something that doesn't feel natural. Of course we are to be honest, but in a relationship, it is honest to live what we *believe*, not what we *feel*. One woman says out of an angry heart: "I can't keep fixing my husband dinner when he comes home late from work and then complains about what I've fixed him. It feels phony," she complains, "to do something I don't feel like doing. Shouldn't I be honest?" She's uncomfortable doing something that is contrary to the way she feels.

It is not phony to live contrary to feelings. Most people do it every morning when they get out of bed even when they are tired, or refuse dessert even when they would like to eat it!

It is phony only to act contrary to *beliefs*. If I believe that love is a worthy value to live by but act insensitive to my mate's needs, I am being phony because I am not acting in accordance with my belief. I am letting my feelings control my life. It is responsible, not phony, to live lovingly even when we do not feel loving. The good news is that, by believing in our love and acting lovingly toward our mate, we will eventually feel the love that we want to feel.

This is not to say that we should squelch negative feelings. It means that *when* we reveal negative feelings it should be done in a constructive and responsible way.

Passion can fluctuate like the wind. It is good to have passionate feelings to motivate us to act lovingly. However, when our passionate feelings have left us, we can restore them by accepting the responsibility to act lovingly toward our mate even though we do not feel like it at the moment.

Paula decided to think about her husband's needs instead of dwelling on her own. In the course of counseling she learned ways to take better care of her own emotional needs so that she wouldn't be overly dependent upon Randy and resentful if he failed her. Then she decided to give to him what she could, even though she felt she wasn't getting much back.

Her first move was to plan and prepare a lovely, candlelight dinner with Randy. During the course of the meal she told her husband what was on her heart:

"Honey, I want you to know that I appreciate all the hard work you do to provide for us. I get lonely for you when you work late, but I know you love me. I just want you to know that I want to be close to you whenever I can be."

Her courage in "singing" her love song by living out her love toward Randy is paying big dividends. Passionate desire is once again present. Most people need to work hard to maintain passion in marriage. We *act* passionate to *feel* passionate. This is the living love song.

We have seen that passion, the emotional dimension of loving, can be powerful and satisfying. But it is a feeling, and as such it is very undependable. True love is more than mere feeling. *Agape* love is behavior governed by our Christian beliefs.

That kind of love doesn't express itself only when it feels good. When we *act* loving, even though we do not *feel* loving, we are fulfilling the command of Christ as well as setting the stage for loving feelings to return to us.

Sounds easy if you say it fast, doesn't it? Let's get specific in the next chapter: *How* can we act loving when we don't feel passionate—or even positive—anymore?

CHAPTER TWO

The Responsible
Love Song

When we choose to live a responsible love song, we assume responsibility for our own attitudes and actions. It is common to blame our partner for how we feel about what they have said to us. But the truth of the matter is that no matter what he or she has done to stimulate our feelings, it is up to us to decide if we will allow that feeling to control our actions, or whether we will take control of our actions regardless of how we feel. The responsible love song does not blame the other, but assumes responsibility for acting with love and self-control. We have discussed that to keep passion alive we must act loving, even when we do not feel like doing so. More specifically, there are at least twelve ways in which we can accept responsibility for this.

1. We can forgive our mate. One of the biggest enemies of positive passion is resentment. When our feelings have been hurt by our mate, it is difficult to get excited about being close. Hurt feelings push us away from those who hurt us. The only passion we can have will be negative and destructive unless we become willing to accept our pain and give up our resentment.

Paula was in pain over Randy's lack of attention. She resented him for this but did not talk about it initially. Paula eventually realized, however, that she needed to talk about it. Once Randy became aware of her feelings, he could do something about it. Paula needed to forgive Randy for his preoccupation with work and allow him the opportunity to understand her needs.

This may seem obvious on the surface, but many of us hold onto our resentments and do not give our spouse a chance to really understand us. Instead of revealing our concern in a kind way, we may become defensive and blaming because we don't really expect our mate to care about us. We are so convinced that our spouses don't care that we don't give them a chance to relate to our concerns. We are afraid of getting hurt again. Fortunately for Paula, she was willing to take the risk with Randy by sharing her feelings, even though it was difficult for her to do so.

If we are to take responsibility for maintaining our desire for closeness to our mate, we must learn to forgive. Forgiveness is one of the most beautiful love songs that we can ever sing. Forgiveness clears the air and presents us with a fresh start. Without forgiveness, we cannot nurture positive passion. By forgiving, we are making a statement that we value our relationship together enough to manage our own pain—for the sake of the relationship. The process of forgiving will be discussed in a subsequent chapter.

2. We can accept our own needs and feelings. Some of us have grown up ignoring our own interests and desires. We were taught to live only for others rather than for ourselves. When this happens, we don't develop a sense of our real self to share with anyone. For passion to exist, we must view our needs and feelings as legitimate. The tension of unmet needs creates desire. If we reject our right to have human needs and feelings, we lose our desire and zest for life.

Paula found support in counseling to accept responsibility for expressing her emotional needs. She became more outspoken about her feelings. This in turn helped her to discover her passionate self, which had "fallen asleep."

As she realized it was okay to ask Randy for attention, she gradually began to feel the return of her desire for him. On one occasion she said, "Randy, I would like to get your reaction to something. When can we have some time to talk together?" His curiosity and response were immediate. "Let's talk now, honey. What's on your mind?"

I once counseled another woman who had put her own needs and feelings "on the shelf" to cater to every whim of her minister husband. She would immediately drop whatever she was doing to respond to his needs. It was never the other way around because she never expressed any needs or interests of her own. The result was that her husband did not feel important to her because he didn't know how to give to an unneedy woman. He began to lose respect for her because she didn't seem to respect herself enough to claim her own needs for emotional support, security, affection, and understanding. There had been no passion in this marriage for over thirty years.

3. We can focus on our mate's positive qualities. For some reason it is easier to take our mate's good qualities for granted and focus on his or her negative traits. How we *think* about our mate is going to affect how we relate to him or her. Although we cannot deny that certain negative characteristics exist, we need not dwell on them. Rather it is more constructive to focus on the good in our mate. This will help us desire to be closer.

I once saw an acting teacher demonstrate to her class how she would play a romantic role with an actor toward whom she had a personal aversion. She looked carefully for one thing about that person that she could physically admire. She decided to focus on his ear. She temporarily focused on how beautiful his ear was to her. When it was time to play the part on camera, you would never have known that she disliked that person. She had a temporary goal as an actress, but we have a more permanent goal of maintaining positive feelings toward our mate. Fixating on our spouse's ear may work for a few minutes on camera. But we need to do more than that for our marriage.

Paula made a list of all of Randy's positive qualities. He was hardworking, understanding, motivated, a good father, and had Christian values. It was helpful for Paula to reflect upon his positive traits.

See how we can influence our feelings when we put our minds to it? We can't wait until it feels "right" or natural. We have to decide what we want and start acting the way we want to feel.

4. We can remember both our good times and our struggles. It is not good to live in the past. We need to be creating new experiences together in our present. Yet occasional reflection upon our history together can rekindle our feelings toward our mate. The laughter, the embarrassing moments, the crises and the struggles we have faced together all can stir our hearts to seek more experiences of togetherness in the present.

Arleen and I enjoy looking back over the years since we moved to Orange County, from Los Angeles. As soon as we were married, her grandmother lived with us for two years. This wasn't exactly how we had planned to spend our first years of marriage. As grandmother declined, it became stressful on both of us. We struggled together about what to do next.

For eighteen months, Arleen commuted seventy miles each way to work in Los Angeles, while I started up my counseling practice in Mission Viejo. It was exhausting, and I hated to see her work so hard, but we had agreed it was the best thing to do for the short term. After we moved, our condominium in Los Angeles sat empty for one year before it sold. To this day I can't figure out how we managed financially. But God worked everything out. Finally Arleen was offered a local job with a sizeable pay increase—which she turned down to go back to school. I was on my knees a lot then. I couldn't imagine going through all that we did without God's help.

Our faith was strong but so was our anxiety. Neither one of us would have attempted all of this alone. But together we work as a team to reach our common goals. Most of what we do is a joint decision from decorating the house to where we will travel.

If we disagree, we either find ways to compromise or we don't move ahead. The tougher the challenge, the harder we support each other and the closer we become. Remembering all of this helps keep our passion for each other alive.

In sharing this story with Paula and Randy in counseling, they began to realize the many experiences that were bonding them together, stimulating their desire to create new and intimate experiences together. Unless we allow ourselves to remember our positive experiences, these memories cannot nurture our passion.

5. We can listen for our mate's love song. Sometimes we get discouraged and lose our passion because we aren't hearing the love song that we are hoping to hear from our mate. We want our mate to love us the way that we think we should be loved. When our expectations aren't met, we feel disappointed.

Paula was so focused upon her need to have Randy's attention that she couldn't hear the love song Randy was already singing to her. Although she had a right to her need for attention, she wasn't initially giving Randy credit for his hard work to provide for her and the family.

Our passion can be restored or enhanced by realizing that our mate really *is* singing a love song, and we simply haven't been hearing it. We can only enjoy a love song when we notice it. So we must listen carefully for what our partner is singing to us and enjoy it for what it is. Do you suppose your mate is singing a love song that you aren't hearing?

We don't have a right to tell our mate what love song to sing. We can ask for what we want, but we must give credit for his or her efforts without judging the limits of the repertoire.

6. We can rejoice in the expression of our own love. God cares about relationships. God is love and love creates relationships. I find it exciting to think that I can participate in God's creative purpose by building a loving relationship with my wife.

Whenever we are building a relationship with love, we are

participating in God's creative purpose. "Love is the fulfillment of the law" (Rom 13:10).

Paula needs and deserves Randy's attention, but she can also find meaning through encouraging Randy in his professional development while also revealing her needs in a kind, non-blaming manner. This is easier to do if she considers how God has given her an amazing opportunity to be a vehicle of his love to Randy.

Thus far, all of the suggestions for increasing passion in ourselves have had to do with how we should *think*. The remaining suggestions have more to do with how we should *behave* toward our mate so that our own desire to be close will remain strong.

7. We can plan to enjoy things together. Our desire to be close to our spouse is enhanced if we think about the other person in the context of doing activities that we both enjoy. It helps our mental attitude toward our spouse to do something together that is exciting or pleasurable. A good example of this may be going on a vacation together. Of course we can't do that every week, but it illustrates taking advantage of the positive emotional association to help us enjoy and move closer to each other.

Although the activity in itself must be something we will enjoy, part of the value of the activity lies in the positive association of an enjoyable time with our partner. Maybe we can borrow someone's cabin in the mountains for a weekend or barbecue steaks at the beach. We might get together with a "passionate" couple from church. Sometimes being around loving people can help us act more loving and outgoing. We can plan outings to a museum, a concert, a sports event, or a scenic spot. We will begin to have something to look forward to doing together. By having fun together, we can rebuild desire for closeness and hope for the future.

An important factor in the success of this exercise is adopting a proper attitude. An openness to trying new behaviors is essential even when it doesn't feel comfortable. One couple went through the motions of going for a drive together because it was something I had recommended. However, they both resented the exercise. Needless to say the exercise didn't improve relations between any of us.

8. We can spend time alone, apart from our spouse. Passion is heightened by separateness. Does that sound like a contradiction? You will notice that when the desire to be close is satisfied, passion tends to decrease temporarily. When we are alone for a period, our desire to be together tends to increase again. Too much closeness can suffocate passion, but time alone can help regenerate our desire for our mate.

I frequently counsel with people who don't seem to enjoy being alone. I am not advocating a hermit lifestyle. However, I believe that until we are comfortable being alone with ourselves, our marriage will be lacking. People who desperately need others around them tend to depend too much on their mate to help them relax.

In counseling Dick, for example, I learned that he does not like living alone. He has been engaged four times in the past six months. He is too anxious to get married. The women to whom he commits himself begin to feel his desperation; all four of them have broken their engagements. What Dick needs to do is develop confidence in himself, that he is an okay person, capable of meeting his own needs, and capable of enjoying a woman in marriage without having to lean on her excessively. When he is comfortable with himself as a single individual, he will have more to bring to the relationship when he does marry.

My wife and I always look forward to seeing each other and sharing our thoughts, feelings, and experiences. However, there are times when we need solitude and are perfectly content to pursue independently our own projects and interests. When we are apart longer than one of us cares to be, we seek each other out.

There is no rigid formula for how much to be together or apart. It depends upon what is best for each of you. The point is that being apart helps build your desire to be together.

9. We can ask for what we want. By asking for what we want, we are increasing the odds of our being satisfied in the relationship. When we have developed a track record of meeting our needs through asking, our affection for our mate increases naturally.

Getting what we want is not the only reason for asking, however. By asking for what we want we are affirming our spouse as having something of value to give, if he or she so chooses.

Asking for what we want doesn't guarantee that we will get it. But if we don't ask, we almost certainly won't get it. Even if we do not get what we want, we have revealed our interest so that our mate can know us a little better.

Asking for what we want affirms our right to have personal desires. Expressing those desires affirms our intention of increased closeness as a couple. Asking trains us to think in terms of our own legitimate needs. If this sounds selfish, it is, but there is a constructive kind of selfishness that is not out to use others or ignore their needs. Constructive selfishness is simply taking responsibility for meeting our own needs.

For example, when Paula goes out with her girlfriends, she leaves her children with a sitter a few hours at a time. This "selfishness" on her part is constructive, because it gives her important time with nurturing friends so that she can better nurture her children when she is with them. By taking responsibility for meeting her own needs, Paula is better able to meet the needs of others.

Sometimes when I come home from work, after listening to people all day, I need more quiet time to wind down than in the ten minutes it takes me to drive home. My wife likes to start talking things over as soon as we see each other. I usually spend a few minutes with her before I tell her I need to do some things in my office for awhile. I let her know that I want to continue discussing things with her and will rejoin her in about thirty minutes. Once I get my head together, being with her is the best part of my day.

My wife is very good at asking for what she wants. She knows that I would give her the moon if I could. But she also knows that I am not in a position to give her everything she wants. She loves me anyway, which makes me want to give her all I can. Asking for what she wants is constructive since she doesn't make demands. Her capacity to want something, yet do without, is a mark of her maturity. By asking, she is revealing to me a little more of who she is.

10. We can give and receive affection. Some of us are, by nature, more affectionate than others. Those of us who are unaffectionate may find it difficult to express our feelings of love and caring openly, but this does not mean that we do not feel passionately. Unfortunately what we do feel doesn't benefit the more affectionate person if it is not openly expressed.

Our present behaviors are a function of past learning. Although it is possible to change behaviors, the conditioned response of our feelings is more than some of us want to tackle. For those of us who are willing to risk the discomfort of expressing affection in ways that may not be natural for us, there is a reward. But it may be slow in coming. People tend to give up on changing their behaviors because it takes too long before they actually feel comfortable expressing affection. However, there is the reward of experiencing new feelings of desire for those who persevere.

Not everyone will be motivated to develop this desire. However, if we have married someone who already had this desire for affection, our responsible love song will make an effort to meet our mate's needs for affection and seek to find enjoyment in it for ourselves as well. We will find that new feelings eventually follow from new behavior.

Of course I am not proposing that we force our affection upon our mate when he or she is not open to it. We must be sensitive to our spouse's feelings or we defeat our purpose. Acting affectionate in the broadest sense toward the other person can, however, have a positive effect on both parties.

We may be encouraged to discover that our expression of affection brings a surprisingly positive response. Even if our mate's response is negative, we have taken a responsible step in demonstrating love. *Agape* love needs no reward for expressing itself.

11. We can affirm our mate's love for us. It is important for our spouses to know that we appreciate their love. We should not take this for granted. By saying it, we are taking a step toward letting ourselves be positively affected by that person's love. This further opens the door for desire to grow within us.

This is what Paula did when she eventually said to Randy, "I appreciate your hard work, Randy, even though I would still like to have more time with you. I know you love me and that is very important to me."

In affirming our mate in this way, we are also reinforcing in our own mind an awareness that we are loved and that there is something of value for us in this relationship. Furthermore, by affirming our mate's love for us we are again accepting our own need for love as valid. The more we accept our need, the more desire we can allow ourselves to feel.

Passion is desire. It stimulates intimacy. Passion is basically selfish, but this desire is a compliment to the beloved who is desired so greatly. Each time we affirm our mate's love, we keep ourselves open to our desire to be close as a couple.

12. We can try to sing our mate's favorite love songs. Although we are free to show our love in our own unique way, we are also free to do some of the loving things that our partner enjoys most. My wife happens to like French bread and a particular brand of chocolate chip ice cream. Some days I will come home with these favorites of hers as a way of letting her know that I think about her. Her preferences are important to me. Bringing her well-chosen gifts is an action that stirs up my loving feelings for her.

What love songs would your mate like to experience from

you? A back rub? A walk on the beach together? Flowers? Planning a weekend away for just the two of you? Calling your mate at work just to say "I love you"? Arranging for the kids to spend the night with their grandparents so you can be alone together?

These loving behaviors, however, should not be done out of our need for approval. This world is too full of people jumping through each other's hoops in order to get a validating response. This is not love. *Agape* love does not give to get.

By singing our mate's favorite love songs, we are acting toward him or her in a caring way simply because we believe in love. Increasingly loving feelings are a side benefit.

If we really want to cultivate passionate feelings in ourselves, we can do it by taking responsibility for our behavior. We can choose to think and act with passion. The difficulty at this point is that most of us are wanting to *feel* passionate before we are willing to act passionately. We want our passion to be a spontaneous, natural occurrence. As we consider acting differently from the way we feel, the internal resistance we experience comes from prior training and habits formed over the years. To break these behavior patterns requires our conscious effort. Eventually, repetition enables us to acquire a new mind-set, which assumes a spontaneity all its own and no longer seems forced or contrived.

This chapter has described twelve ways we can purposefully cultivate marital passion—in ourselves. To improve any marriage, we must begin with ourselves. This is the responsible love song. Only after we have formed new habits and firmed up our own intention to cultivate passion in our marriage, are we ready to consider ways to encourage passion in our mate. This will be our consideration in the next chapter.

CHAPTER THREE

The Encouraging
Love Song

Paula was alone when she came to my office for one session. She had been working with some success on developing her own feelings of passion. Now she wanted to know what she could do to encourage Randy to become more passionate. Because of her own success with herself, she was hopeful that he also could develop a greater desire for mutual intimacy.

There is a difference between actively trying to change our mate and creating an environment that promotes whatever growth he or she may wish to experience. If we are seeking ways for our partner to become more passionate, we are wise to lead the way rather than to make demands on the other person. If we have the proper attitude of setting an example and showing appreciation for our mate's loving behaviors, we can support him or her in the direction of demonstrating more passion. Our mate needs to feel accepted or we will meet with resistance. We must not manipulate the people just to please ourselves.

What can we specifically do then, to encourage our partners in becoming more passionate—without nagging, which would only undermine our purpose? Here are twelve positive approaches.

1. We can develop our own passion. Attitudes can be catching. If we set an example with our own life, we are communicating that passion is important to us. Furthermore, we may well stimulate him or her into responding in a pleasing way if we can demonstrate passion without blaming our mate for being less passionate than we would like. It is important to take a kind of joy in our own passionate behavior that is independent of our partner's validating response. If we enjoy our passion, so might our mate.

Although it made her feel a little vulnerable, Paula was willing to reveal her own passion with Randy. She initiated "date night" and planned activities they could both enjoy doing together. She talked openly about her feelings and asked him questions to help him do the same.

If we want to encourage passion in our husband or wife, we need to take responsibility for letting our own passion show. It may seem easier to wait for the other person to take the lead, but taking the initiative ourselves is an outgrowth of developing our own passion.

2. We can be sensitive to our mate's physical and emotional needs. We sing our love song by paying attention to our mate's priorities and preferences. In all likelihood, we prefer different kinds of physical activity or emotional expression from each other. For that reason, we need to try to find a balance, so that both of us can find some satisfaction. However, we must make sure we are paying close enough attention to our beloved to know what his or her needs and preferences really are.

Randy, for example, works hard, comes home tired and brain dead from problem-solving all day. He is running scared at work to keep ahead of his competition and is worried about their personal finances. By being sensitive to Randy's concerns, Paula can encourage in him feelings of desire toward her. She might prepare meals she knows he enjoys, massage his sore muscles, play his favorite music, praise him for his qualities, or offer to get a part-time job.

How can we become more sensitive to another's needs? What kinds of needs are there? Some of us like to have time alone to think while others prefer frequent socializing. Some need the security of time to plan events while others prefer to be more spontaneous. Some are physically active; others are more sedentary. Some like to receive a lot of external stimulation while others prefer to be the stimulators. Some like routine while others prefer variety.

Take, for example, George and Mary. They came in for counseling because they were constantly fighting. Their most recent fight was over their vacation. Mary wanted every detail planned in advance. She doesn't like surprises. On the other hand George likes the freedom to be spontaneous and do what he feels like doing at the moment. Overplanning ruins a vacation for him. The only solution was to reveal these feelings and come to a compromise. When each of them discovered that they cared about the other's feelings and strong preferences, they felt more passionate toward each other than when they thought the other didn't care. Antagonism was reduced.

What makes it difficult sometimes is that people don't always know what they need. In cases like this we have to observe our mate over a period of time to see what needs they manifest unconsciously. For example, Mary feels insecure about being loved, so she wants reassurance of being loved by seeking George's attention. If George were to ask himself why she wants so much of his attention, he might recognize that Mary has a high need for reassurance. By being sensitive to this and giving her what she needs, he would be encouraging her feelings of passion toward him.

3. We can pursue personal interests independent of our mate. I am not suggesting that we put all of our time into this. Yet there are definite advantages for couples not being together constantly. For one thing, it gives both a chance to miss each other so our desire to be close can grow and intensify once again.

Of course being apart, whether it is a matter of hours or days, does not guarantee that we will miss our mate. We have to have a stable and committed relationship for this to work. Assuming the marriage is fairly stable, being apart "to make the heart grow fonder" can be a helpful way to promote passion. Too much time apart can discourage a relationship, but too much closeness can kill passion, too.

Having different personal activities will give us something to discuss with each other when we are together. We will be more stimulating and appealing to our mate when we each can initiate conversation regarding our feelings and experiences.

In addition, just being alone from time to time is important for processing our own thoughts and bringing peaceful resolution to some of our personal concerns. When our mind is clear of loose ends from the day, and we have had time to organize our plan for tomorrow, we will be more relaxed with our partner and probably sleep better too.

Of course, if we are absent from each other too much and lose hope of ever being close, then the relationship can fall apart. How much time a couple can constructively handle apart from each other varies from couple to couple. Some people are capable of travelling on the job all week and only seeing each other on the weekends. Others are separated due to military service for months at a time. At the other extreme are couples who hate to be apart for even one day.

Problems can develop when the husband and wife have opposite needs for time together. Paula needs frequent contact with Randy, whereas Randy could function quite well if he had to be gone on business for a week. He would miss his family and would speak to them on the phone a few times, but he wouldn't be as uncomfortable as Paula would be. The solution to this kind of problem is for each to sing a love song of understanding and caring compromise. If Randy were on a business trip, he could phone Paula more frequently. Paula, on the other hand could refrain from complaining to Randy. Instead she could say to him, "I miss you, honey. I am glad you care enough to call me. It means a lot to me."

4. We can laugh and play together. Imagine how different things would be at home if you acted a little silly once in a while. Laughter always feels good, unless of course we've just come out of surgery. Our ability to make our mate laugh is almost guaranteed to increase his or her desire for us. I believe that our ability to laugh, even all by ourselves, produces a healthier environment.

My wife slept in one morning, so I decided to fix her a special breakfast. I knew she liked eggs benedict, but I didn't have the slightest idea how they were made. So I asked her. She enthused, "muffin, ham, poached egg, and Hollandaise sauce!" I didn't even know what Hollandaise sauce was and I was sure we didn't have any of it in the house. Furthermore, we didn't have any of the ingredients needed except for the egg. So, I decided to be creative. I toasted a piece of French bread, poached us each an egg, and boiled two hot dogs and sliced them up to take the place of the ham. I probably should have stopped there but I didn't want to appear ignorant about that whatchamacallit sauce. So I opened a can of chicken à la king sauce and poured it over the rest of this wonderful breakfast. Well, for some reason I liked it better than she did! I ate all of my portion and most of hers. She said she wasn't very hungry (as she surveyed the refrigerator contents). I thought I would be generous and share a bit with our dog. I guess the dog wasn't hungry either.

Now I'm not known for keeping people in stitches laughing, but I had fun that morning whether she did or not. It is good for a marriage, even if only one of us is having a good time, as long as it isn't at our mate's expense. This is better than nobody having any fun. We all like to be around happy people. We can't expect our mate always to be "up" to make us happy, but taking responsibility for our own happiness and fun might increase his or her desire to be close to us.

I have a friend who makes me laugh without even trying. As much as I enjoy his humor, I get an even bigger kick out of watching his wife respond to him. She watches him the way a little kid watches a magician. The "what's he gonna say next?" look on her face tells me she enjoys her husband and has a strong desire to be close to him. I believe his humor fuels her passion for him.

We can't all be natural comedians, but we can work at having a sense of humor. Although we need our time for serious sharing, humor can generate passion. Having a sense of humor is not the same as being a practical joker. Jokes and surprises can be fun, but it isn't wise to do them unless you know your partner will enjoy them. Practical jokes generally are not compatible with intimacy. If jokes are needed to maintain a level of interest in the relationship, chances are there is no true intimacy. Practical jokes are frequently rooted in the fear of intimacy, and the only thing passionate about them is the intense desire to avoid being known at a deeply personal level. Practical jokes played on one's mate can undermine passion severely. Women especially want to feel secure in a relationship and not have to worry about keeping their guard up for "surprises."

5. We can be dependable. We all like the security of knowing we can count on others. This means following through with promises and commitments. Being dependable provides a sense of stability and security which is very important to any relationship. When our mate knows we can be relied upon, he or she will feel more trusting and safe to be close to us. Are you as dependable as you might be with your mate? What does your mate rely upon you to do? Fix meals? Service the cars? Go to the market? Pick up the cleaning? Pay the bills on time? Show up when and where you promise? Of course, dependability should be a two-way street. But we are discussing how we can sing our love song in a way that will heighten our mates passion for us. Dependability makes us desirable.

6. We can keep ourselves appealing. It is easy to get caught up in routines and become lazy about ourselves. Over the years of married life we may easily gain weight, get less exercise, sleep in dirty pajamas, and start taking on other bad habits. Tanya was offended because her husband Mike sucked his toothpaste directly out of the tube. You can almost guess how he dressed. A sloppy T-shirt hanging out over his pot belly did not stir her passion in the least.

Ted would come to the dinner table looking sloppy and smelling like a "dead lizard." (I am taking his wife's word on this.) When Sheila asked him to clean up a little for her he said it was too much trouble. She then explained that he was free to dress as he wished in his own house, but she was also free to eat where she didn't have to look at him. Sheila excused herself politely and took her meal out onto the patio to eat. The next meal Ted was cleaned up.

It is not only a matter of respect to be appealing to our spouse. It is also a matter of good sense to attract each other with our confidence, self-respect, and positive energy.

Randy was so caught up in his work that his emotional needs were not being satisfied. He ate excessively between meals and was gaining quite a bit of weight. This was a concern of Paula's. She didn't want his weight to be a significant factor in her love for him, but it did make it difficult for her to want to be close to him. As he began to pay more attention to her, his weight became less of a problem for her. Since his emotional needs were also being better satisfied, he started to lose weight.

Mutual appeal can be enhanced not only through maintaining a pleasant appearance, but also by way of implementing the suggestions in this and the previous chapter. Acting passionately, being sensitive to our mate, laughing, being positive, affirming, affectionate, straightforward, taking initiative, and so forth are all ways of promoting our appeal to each other.

7. We can help our mate feel appreciated. The obvious way for us to do this is to *tell* our mate that we appreciate him or her. There must be a million ways to communicate this. Arleen and I usually have an instant smile on our face as soon as we see each other.

I was in the neighborhood near her office one day so I stopped in for a few minutes to see her. She was on the phone so we didn't get to talk. Nevertheless she felt important to me because I went out of my way to see her. I felt important to her when I saw her smile as I walked into her office. That was all either of us needed.

We can give compliments and praise. "I appreciate your doing the laundry for me, dear," is one example. Another is, "I sure like being married to you."

Another way to affirm our spouse is to say something positive about him or her in public or to friends. We shouldn't make up things that are not true. However, we can show our mate our esteem by sharing praise with others. Over the course of time, it is these little things that will make a difference in our marriage.

The biggest hurdle is that we tend to let our negative feelings control us. It is our choice whether we will let our anger win or whether we will take charge of our behavior and turn a negative into a positive.

8. We can ask for what we want without being critical. This sounds so simple but often gets overlooked. However, after twenty-five years as a marriage counselor, I can declare that this is worth your careful consideration. Nearly all of us in our own way at some time use our past experience to put down our spouse. Yet all we really want is to have a more positive experience in the future.

Paula used to make statements like "Aren't you ever going to learn that I don't like sweets?" or "You never think about what I might like to do before you buy tickets!" These are blaming statements based upon past experiences, which no one can change. Needless to say, these kinds of blaming statements simply pushed Randy further away from her.

Blaming statements will surely dampen our sweetheart's passionate desire to be close to us. Yet a simple statement of request in the present tense, even if said previously, can make a tremendous difference in our communication.

How can we rephrase the above blaming statements into positive, present requests? "Thanks for the candy, Randy. It pleases me that you think about me when I am not around. But I am not much of a sweets eater. I wish you would bring me flowers sometime." (Of course, our tone of voice is important too. If we say this with a whine, we won't get very far!)

As I write, I can hear some of you react to this. "Are you kidding? You expect me to be that direct? If I said that, I would be told to get lost!" If this is your reaction, you just may need to pay special attention to this recommendation. Some of us don't believe we have a right to ask for what we want. We fail to respect ourselves enough to make personal requests. If we want to be respected by our mate, we must treat ourselves with respect. Even if he or she says "nuts to you," we have made a firm and kind statement about what we would prefer, without being demanding. Even if we meet with resistance at the moment, we still might get what we want later.

Another way to respond positively is to say, "I am glad you took the initiative to invite me out. Maybe next time I could participate with you in picking out the event."

Asking for what we want doesn't mean we will get it. But it's a positive step which can increase our partner's interest in us.

9. We can encourage our mate. To encourage means to inspire confidence in another through reassurance and cheerful support. It means to believe in our mate when he or she cannot. Many times when one of us is discouraged, we try to solve the other's problems with advice. For the most part, advice is not synonymous with encouragement.

We need to support our spouse. We usually can't solve the problems anyway, but we can be an encouragement and demonstrate tender loving care and quiet confidence.

We all want to feel that others are behind us. When we are given the confidence that our spouse is supportive of us, we tend to feel positive toward him or her. If we encourage our mate, we build trust and desire in them to be close to us.

When Arleen and I moved to Orange County, the transition was a bumpy one. As I was attempting to build a private practice from nothing, she was supportive and encouraging. She believed in me when I got discouraged. I like immediate gratification and was disillusioned when my phone wasn't ringing off the hook. And I had been "open for business" for a whole month! But Arleen was reassuring and encouraging that things would build in time. And so they did.

It wasn't long, however, before the shoe was on the other foot. When Arleen began commuting daily seventy miles each way to seminary, she needed my encouragement. As a dyslexic, she suffered through Greek and Hebrew with my support. I also typed her papers for her (before I got my first computer). We didn't have a lot of time together in those days, but typing her papers at least helped us feel connected at some level. Supporting her in her endeavor was one way of encouraging her.

Knowing that we are really there for each other through difficult times keeps alive our desire for each other. Encouragement is another one of those choices that we may not always feel like offering. However, if we want to stir up passion in our partner, we will seek to be encouraging.

10. We can balance talking with listening. Obviously both talking and listening are important. But most of us tend to be better at one than the other. Couples who have a balance between talking and listening have a better chance at feeling mutually important. Few couples are perfectly balanced in this regard. A woman who talks 60 percent of the time to a husband who talks the other 40 percent (no stereotype intended) is actually pretty balanced. But when the man, for example, does 90 percent of the talking, this could undermine the potential for passion in the relationship. Why is this?

Since marital passion is the desire to be close to our mate, there has to be some means for that desire to grow. In order to desire closeness, we have to sense that our mate cares about us, understands us, and accepts us. Now, if we aren't saying much, we have fewer chances to feel cared about, understood, and accepted. If we are the one doing all the talking, we may be wearing down our mate and diminishing their passion by not giving them equal attention.

It is difficult to sustain a passionate desire to be close to our mate when we do not sense our mate's involvement with us. I find it amazing how some "talkers" are oblivious to their mate's uninvolvement with them. They chatter on and on as if their spouse is digesting every word. I think in many cases our incessant talking is just to distract us from our anxiety and pain over our inability to connect.

In any case, it would be helpful to encourage our quieter partner's participation by talking less in order to show interest in him or her. "How was your day?" "How do you feel about what happened?" "What did you like the best? the least?" "What would you like from me right now?" Compliment your mate on something. Tell how you are feeling toward him or her at the moment. Give your spouse a chance to speak about whatever seems important.

If we want to encourage passion in our mate, we can balance talking with listening so both of us can feel an equal part of the relationship.

11. We can make decisions together. "You did *what?!*" Paula screamed. Randy thought Paula would be delighted with the new Buick he brought home. But she was furious because she was not part of that decision process. Buying a car is not only a big decision for most people but an exciting one. Paula needed to feel that this was her car also. She would like to have had something to say about the color and model they chose. Randy expected Paula to be excited by his surprise. She got excited all right, but not the way he expected. Had he included her in the decision, they could have felt closer from having shared a satisfying joint decision.

Decision-making is an expression of our inner self. When we

make decisions with our mate, we are engaged together at a very personal level. Randy's exclusion of Paula from this decision robbed them both of the joy of mutual participation.

12. We can be comforting. To comfort means to calm or soothe. This may not sound like a very passionate activity but it creates an environment in which passion can grow. When our mate feels comforted by us with some consistency over time, he or she will feel good about the relationship and be more inclined to participate. By making your mate feel good by offering personal comfort, you stimulate a passionate desire for more comfort. This, in turn, often creates a desire for more of *you.*

Listen attentively, showing interest in what your mate is saying. Sometimes giving your spouse some time alone to unwind from a hard day would be comforting. A back rub might be enjoyable. Perhaps serving your loved one breakfast in bed would be of comfort. Showing comfort is as personal as all the other ways of singing your love song of encouragement.

These are all ways we can help generate passion in our mate. They are all love songs of encouragement. As we support each other, we are helping to keep our love alive.

It is important to remember that love songs are not to be sung for the purpose of manipulating what we want from our beloved. Although it is reasonable to hope that our mate would be responsive to us, our primary motivation should be out of our own desire to act lovingly toward him or her. Then we can enjoy the positive self-esteem that comes from knowing we are doing what is good and loving in the eyes of our Heavenly Father.

These first three chapters have emphasized that marital passion is the desire to be close to our mate. Furthermore, even when we do not feel like it, it is still our privilege and our responsibility to pursue closeness with our partner. When we take responsibility for our behavior by thinking in loving terms and by acting in loving ways toward our husband or our wife, we can actually generate loving feelings in ourselves. By acting the way we want to feel, we can eventually feel the way we are acting.

I have suggested some behaviors that can assist in developing these feelings of passion in our marriage. This involves cultivating passion in ourselves as well as encouraging passionate feelings in our mate. It is vital to take responsibility for keeping passion alive in our marriage, even when we might not feel like it.

If marital passion is the desire for closeness—intimacy—with our mate, how do we satisfy that desire? What makes the conversion from unresolved desire to full-fledged intimacy? The fulfillment of marital passion is explored in the next section as we consider the love song of intimacy.

SECTION II

The Love Song of Intimacy

CHAPTER FOUR

The Intimate
Love Song

Joe is a forty-seven-year-old engineer with a computer manufacturer. He was referred to me for counseling because he was "not happy with how things were going at home." When I asked him to be more specific, it became clear that Joe and Donna were merely going through the motions; there was no real intimacy in their relationship.

They both seemed to be spending increasing amounts of time at work. She had taken a night job in a department store when Joe was home to watch the children. Donna didn't have to work but she did it for the personal contact with others. Joe is a responsible, conscientious person who works hard to provide for his family. However, the discomfort at home motivated him to travel on the weekends "for work purposes."

Joe is an introverted type of person who has always preferred having time to himself. However, when he was home with Donna and tried to be close to her, she just moved away from him. What little conversation they did have was disconnected, impersonal, and businesslike. Although Joe wanted intimacy with his wife, he didn't know how to achieve it.

"I am so confused," said Joe. "I make a good living. I give the children my attention. I always let Donna have her way. I just want to make her happy. Yet Donna says I don't give of myself. What am I not giving?"

"I can see why this is so confusing for you, Joe," I responded. "On the one hand you love Donna and you want to make her happy. But it seems like you have done all you know how to do in order to please her, and she just becomes more distant."

"That's right! It doesn't make any sense!" he said.

Actually, what was happening in Joe's life made a lot of sense. Joe was just viewing things from the wrong angle. He did not feel close to Donna because he did not know how to be intimate. Intimacy comes from mutual self-disclosure, not from performing for each other. Wanting to please each other is a good thing, but doing it to earn approval from our partner is not the basis for closeness.

What is really going on here? Why can't Joe and Donna find the intimacy they would both really like to have between them?

Donna has her own point of view about their relationship. "Joe is indecisive and unsure of what he wants," she said. "He seemed stronger and more in charge when we first met. Now he seems so tentative and unsure of himself. He doesn't get involved with what I say. He does almost everything I ask, but he never asks anything of me. I don't feel important to him anymore. I don't even feel like I know him. I just don't understand him."

Joe thought that if he could do everything Donna wanted, he could make her happy, she would accept him, and they could be intimate. But intimacy is not yielding to our mate's requests. Intimacy is giving our mate *who we are*. It is revealing our true selves to each other, not pretending to be who we think the other wants us to be. Intimacy is being real and open.

Joe is afraid to be himself with Donna, even after being married ten years. This may sound strange, but Joe has never felt comfortable being himself around anyone. He feels guilty thinking about his own needs when he is around Donna. What he needs to realize is that Donna wants to know her husband in a very personal way.

Marital intimacy is detailed knowledge of each other. Donna needs to know what is important to Joe and what his needs really are. Without this understanding she cannot know how to give to him. She must know him intimately before she can respond to his needs and feel that she has a significant part to play in his life. Although Joe wants to make her happy, in reality he is making both of them miserable by not revealing himself. At present, it is less painful for her to pull away from him than to move toward his unrevealing self. She feels less lonely when he is at work than she does when he is at home.

Joe thinks the only time he can have his own life is to go quietly within himself, withdraw from others, and enjoy his thoughts and fantasies. It doesn't occur to Joe that his wife would like to share his private inner world with him. Like the Lone Ranger, he does good things for people while hiding behind a mask so nobody can know him. "Who is that masked man I am married to?" she asks.

Donna has a very different personality, so it has been difficult for her to understand Joe's behavior. She has felt hurt, rejected, and emotionally abandoned by the very one who claims to love her. Donna has assumed that Joe was deliberately shutting her out of his life. In one sense that was true. However, it never occurred to her that he didn't really know how to relate to her any differently. She could have helped the marriage if she had taken the responsibility to talk to him about her concerns much earlier in their relationship.

How can Joe and Donna learn to sing a love song of intimacy to each other?

PASSION AND INTIMACY

Marital intimacy is personal familiarity between a husband and wife. It is sharing personal details with each other. In general, intimacy is being close to our mate as a result of mutual self-disclosure and acceptance.

Marital passion is the *desire* for closeness. Intimacy is the *fulfillment* of that desire. Imagine that you are hungry. You have a "passion" for food until you have taken your fill at the table. Your "intimacy" with food has satiated you and diminished your passion for food temporarily. But your hunger will return if you go for a time without eating.

So it is with emotional closeness. As intimacy is achieved, passion declines temporarily. Likewise when intimacy has been absent for a period, our appetite (passion) again returns. Desire and fulfillment must alternate with each other. We desire something because we don't yet have it. Fulfillment diminishes our desire. This alternation does not go on and off like a light switch. Rather it is more like a rheostat—passionate desire fades out as intimate fulfillment is being realized. Likewise when intimacy has been absent for a period, passion again begins to build. It is this repeated sequence of passion alternating with intimacy that is the heartbeat of a healthy relationship.

If a relationship gets stuck in either position, it becomes unhealthy. For example, the marriage that experiences only passion without the fulfillment of intimacy will eventually die. Passion needs hope to survive. If passion does not lead to intimate fulfillment eventually the individual becomes frustrated and despairing.

On the other hand, if the relationship gets stuck on the intimate side, passionate desire cannot be felt, and the relationship becomes boring, stagnates, and will eventually die. Thus it is vital to any loving relationship to experience both passion and intimacy on a regular, but alternating basis.

Joe and Donna's passion was cooling down because it wasn't finding the intimate expression it required for fulfillment. Over time, as we shall see, they learned to sing an intimate love song to each other which helped give birth to their passion once again.

INTIMACY IS NOW

There is more to understand about intimacy, however, than its relationship to passion. Intimacy must be viewed as a present experience. This means that a couple cannot find intimacy on their honeymoon and expect that memory to satisfy them years later. Positive memories are important and beneficial. However, the desire for intimacy keeps coming back. Memories of previous intimate moments may help stimulate our desire to be close again. But the need for intimacy is never satisfied once and for all. Intimacy must be renewed through new experiences together in the present moment.

It is not necessary or desirable for every moment together to be an intimate moment. We need to have *un*intimate moments in order to renew our passion. It is the absence of intimacy as well as positive experiences with intimacy that create the desire. Since intimacy can only be experienced in the present moment, however, it must be recreated on a regular basis in order to sustain a relationship.

Some people talk a lot about past or future activities but say very little about what they are thinking or feeling in the present. The most intimate experience we can have is to share our deepest personal feelings toward our mate in the present moment.

THE PACE OF INTIMACY

Intimacy develops gradually. Many people are so hungry for intimacy that they want it immediately. Some make the mistake of thinking that sexual openness will relieve their loneliness more quickly than working at developing true intimacy. This path is taken by many who do not know any other way. Detailed knowledge and personal familiarity with another person cannot occur instantaneously because it takes time and effort to be openly communicative and mutually accepting.

THE MUTUALITY OF INTIMACY

Intimacy is reciprocal. I have on occasion accompanied people to meetings of Alcoholics Anonymous. It is fascinating to hear the stories of people who have been possessed by alcohol and how they have struggled to stay sober. However, it has been equally fascinating for me to see how people respond to speakers who have just told their life story in personal detail.

After the meetings, listeners gather around the speaker with gratitude and admiration. They feel like they know this person who has just revealed so much detail about himself or herself. I am sure the speaker enjoys the attention but there is no intimate relationship at that moment because the listeners have not shared their lives in any depth with the speaker. Although the listeners are greatly helped by knowing the speaker better, the intimacy is not mutual. Everyone at the meeting has something in common, but of course reciprocal relating is not their purpose. The listeners feel close to the speaker because the speaker was open and self-disclosing. However, the speaker cannot feel close to the members of the audience unless they also disclose, which is not practical in this kind of setting. For people to have a truly intimate experience, disclosure must be reciprocal.

One person opening up to another is only the beginning of intimate relating. Joe would listen to Donna, but because he did not know how to reciprocate, Donna pulled away in despair.

STEPPING STONES TO INTIMACY

Intimacy involves the whole person. Knowing each other is not just a cognitive experience. An intimate marriage is one in which our total personalities are involved. This includes our thoughts, our feelings, and our actions.

Joe thought he was being loving by doing a lot of things that he believed would make Donna happy. However, he never shared his intentions with Donna so that she could relate to him about them. If Joe had said at some point that he was trying to do things to make her happy but she just seemed to keep pulling away, this could have created an intimate moment. This very act of sharing his personal thoughts is an effort to be intimate.

Joe could have said, "Donna, I feel *discouraged* about what to do for our relationship. It *hurts* me to feel so *ineffective* in meeting your needs. I really *desire* a closer relationship with you."

Some people initiate more intimacy with their pets than they do with their mates. They can call their puppy a little sweetheart but they don't do it with their own spouse. Yet verbally sharing our own feelings *about* each other *to* each other is important for the development of intimacy.

Intimacy involves actions. What we think or feel has little consequence if it is not translated into behavior. True intimacy cannot stop with just a thought or a feeling. An intimate moment is created by the process of sharing, selectively, that thought or feeling.

If Joe had revealed his concerns, bought Donna her favorite perfume, or revealed more of his own needs, he would have paved the way for a more intimate relationship. On the other hand, had Donna expressed her concern more directly rather than withdrawing, fixed Joe his favorite meal once in a while, and acted lovingly even when she didn't feel like it, she also might have paved the way to greater intimacy with him.

INTIMACY AND ONENESS

The night before their wedding, a bride-to-be said to her intended, "Just think, dear. Tomorrow the two of us shall become one."

"Oh yeah?" he responded. "Which one?"

"Two becoming one" does not mean one becoming swallowed up by the other. Some of us think that to be intimate we have to think alike, feel the same, and do everything together all the time. If we lose our identity to another, we have little to give each other.

It is our uniqueness that our mate finds so interesting. It is our autonomy that enables us to bring our distinct self to our mate by choice and desire rather than out of need or fear of being alone.

It is a lot easier if spouses share similar values, especially in relation to God, but we don't have to prepare meals the same way or read the same magazines to be intimate. Intimacy is not merging two personalities into one. Rather, it is retaining our own uniqueness and revealing it to each other. Marital intimacy is knowing each other inside out.

Fred and Jan are in their fifties. He is a social worker and she is a supermarket cashier. They were both raised to give themselves away to other people but were not shown how to nurture themselves as well. They were both highly respected in the church for all the time they devoted to church projects. They were humble people who were always there behind the scenes helping out. They shared a lot of their interest in giving, and many people benefited. However, they were like soldiers who worked side by side to meet the needs of the world. There was no intimacy because their own thoughts, feelings, and needs were never revealed to each other. Neither one of them initiated anything on their own behalf. They were both responders to the needs and interests of others. Because they never revealed their own needs and desires, they could not respond to each other. There was nothing to respond to. So they kept busy looking beyond each other for needs to which they could respond. They are always side by side but seldom eye to eye.

Their marriage is faltering now because they are burning out. Their cups are empty. They have gone through the motions of giving all their lives when in fact they had very little to give due to their self-imposed emotional deprivation. Without knowing how to nurture themselves by having fun and learning how to relax, they became caught in a dangerous routine of giving to everyone except themselves.

When I ask Fred what he would like for himself, he can only answer in terms of what he thinks Jan needs. He does not know himself well enough to define his own needs and interests. The same is true of Jan. She is so used to centering her life around Fred that she has no idea what her own needs are.

Isn't marriage about giving more than getting? Yes! Marriage is very much about giving, both to our mate and to ourselves. Isn't this the ideal marriage? No! If we expect to have resources with which to give, we must receive as well. If a stream is to produce water without drying up, it must have a source of input as well.

If we are unaware of our needs, these needs are not likely to be met. Fred and Jan didn't realize how important it was for each of them to have their respective time alone to think and pray. Fred and Jan are so enmeshed in each other's lives that they have no life of their own with which to share with each other. They bring no fresh perspectives or unique experiences to their relationship.

THE SIGNIFICANCE OF INTIMACY

It seems apparent that most people want to be close to someone else. But why is this so? What motivates us to seek closeness with another?

True intimacy makes us feel accepted and loved. We all have a desire to feel significant and it is most reassuring when another person considers us worthy of close personal involvement. Acceptance by another person reassures us that we have something to offer another. It gives our life meaning and purpose.

We can only love someone to the extent that we know them. Since intimacy is a state of knowing another, it opens the door for personalized expressions of love. As we become more aware of who our marital partner is and what his or her needs are, we learn what love songs are most appropriate to sing. For example, if we realize that our loved one has a fear of heights, we aren't going to plan a trip to the Empire State Building. Or if we know our spouse is allergic to cats, we will not surprise our beloved with a gorgeous Siamese at Christmas.

Intimacy enables us to be mutually sensitive to each other's needs. One of the ways God desires to reveal his love to us is through each other.

Love is essentially behavior. No matter how much we think or feel loving, these loving thoughts and feelings are worthless until translated into behavior. This loving behavior is made more possible through the detailed knowledge that comes from intimate relating. Because intimacy reveals needs, the greater the intimacy, the greater the potential is for love to be demonstrated.

This is not to say that love is going to be expressed simply because intimacy is present. Intimacy provides the opportunity for love but not the assurance of it. Many people have gotten themselves into destructive relationships and have been hurt by being too intimate with the wrong person. So while intimacy does not promise love, it opens the door for healthy love to express itself.

As Christians, we are commanded to love God and one another. The *agape* love that Jesus commands us to live has nothing to do with how we feel. We act loving toward God and others because that is the purpose given to us by our Creator. We are to love as a way of life, not just when it is safe. At times it may be painful to be loving. Nevertheless, an attitude of love should motivate our actions. God never allows pain to be an excuse for not loving. We are called to demonstrate our love regardless of how we feel or how much we are hurting. Even if we have to flee for our lives or leave our spouse to find safety from his or her loss of self-control, we are still exhorted to forgive and be concerned for our mate's emotional and spiritual recovery.

Our personal fulfillment in this life comes primarily in loving God and each other. This is the purpose for which we were created. This is the frame of reference Jesus taught and lived throughout his life on earth. This is the touchpoint which can give our life meaning and direct us in making decisions in our daily lives.

Marital intimacy is a wonderful opportunity for us to fulfill God's purpose in our lives. It is our chance to sing a love song to our mate as well as to God.

OBSTACLES TO INTIMACY

As important as intimacy is to a marriage, it is not always easily achieved. There are several reasons why intimacy can be elusive.

Some of us are afraid to let our spouse know too much about ourselves. We may be afraid something we say may be used against us in the future. Or maybe we don't care for our mate's immediate response. But protecting ourselves from potential hurt and disappointment only sets us up for the pain of loneliness and loss of intimacy. By hiding, we undermine the possibility of closeness because we are not giving our mate anything of ourselves to know and love. This creates a dissatisfied spouse and produces the very thing we fear in the first place: criticism and lack of appreciation.

Fear of being hurt is the main risk of intimacy. Those of us who are afraid to be known usually have a good reason. At some point in our personal history we were hurt. So we protect ourselves by hiding, but only end up being lonely.

Some people respond to their fear by trying to control everything. They feel a need for power in a relationship because they have not been free in previous relationships. We easily confuse power and freedom. We are mistaken to think that to insure our freedom we have to control others. We do not need to control others in order to not be controlled by them. We can set boundaries regarding how we are affected by our mate without becoming a dictator. When one spouse tries to control the other, it develops into a never-ending power struggle. Power over another only creates distrust and resentment. Marital intimacy requires reciprocal freedom rather than one-sided mastery. Power plays will mute any love song.

Actually there is more personal power in *not* controlling our mate. Control undermines the other's loving initiative. But the power of patience opens the door for love to enter on its own. What greater experience is there than to be loved by another's free choice?

Ron is a very high-energy person. Since his wife's illness she has become a very low-energy person. His irritation over this causes him to act impatiently and pushy with her. He believes she should be over her illness by now and should push herself harder to play tennis and go places with him. But love cannot be mandated!

He cheats himself with his demands. Ron's need to be in control interferes with whatever love songs his wife might have been inclined to sing. Even if he succeeds in persuading her to go boating with him, the outing will not satisfy him because the decision did not come from her heart.

We are motivated in our efforts to control our mate by our insecurity about our own lovableness. The irony is that trying to make our spouse love us on our terms causes the other person to withdraw. If we would just accept our lovability as a fact (regardless of how we feel) we would be in a better place to receive the love we want and need.

In this chapter we have considered that marital intimacy is a process of mutual self-disclosure between a husband and wife. It requires time to develop, and it must be reciprocal, involving our thoughts, feelings, and behaviors. True intimacy is an oft-repeated, present experience, not a distant memory. Intimacy is sharing our uniqueness rather than being enmeshed with each other at the expense of our own personal identity. Intimacy opens the door for loving by revealing mutual needs for each other's loving response. Although there are reasons why intimacy is difficult to achieve, it is a significant ingredient in a marriage relationship.

Let us now return to the very important foundational building block for marital intimacy—personal autonomy. Each of us must first know how to sing a solo before trying a duet.

CHAPTER FIVE

The Autonomous Love Song

Ginger and Bud were childhood sweethearts. Bud was student body president and captain of the football team. He dated half the girls in school but he always had a special feeling for Ginger. She was the cheerleader whom Bud had always adored. They were married when they were twenty.

Bud was always self-confident and independent, and Ginger tended to rely on Bud a lot. Her parents had always been good to her, but she had also relied on them instead of taking risks and pursuing life on her own. She was a compliant and responsive person, but always seemed to need others to take the initiative. Ginger was totally reliable on routine matters with which she was familiar. But she was afraid to make decisions on her own or initiate new activities.

Bud and Ginger had been married ten years when they first appeared in my office. Since their marriage, Bud had graduated from college and was working his way up the corporate ladder of a computer manufacturing company. His latest promotion had made quite an impact on their marriage because it required considerable traveling.

"I don't see why Bud has to be gone so much," cried Ginger. "He never had to do it before. There must be something else he could do at work so he wouldn't have to be gone from me so much."

Ginger didn't know how to adjust to her new circumstances, so she looked for Bud to do the adjusting. Although Bud was usually the one to accommodate her needs, this time he was not able to do so without quitting his job and starting over somewhere else—where the same problem could arise again later anyway.

Ginger continued to elaborate. "The children seem to fight more when Bud is out of town. I am afraid the car will break down on me with Bud gone, so I don't go anywhere. I feel lonely not having any friends to talk to. I feel trapped and frightened. And when the water heater began to leak, that was the last straw. I knew I needed Bud to be home with me. This job is disrupting our whole marriage."

Ginger wasn't able to see her alternatives because she had not developed her own autonomy. She had never had to make major adjustments before and therefore lacked confidence in her ability to do so. Without Bud's support within reach, she was afraid to try anything on her own. Her lack of experience in taking care of herself made this abrupt transition very difficult for her.

"I can see why you are so upset, Ginger. It must seem overwhelming to you," I responded.

"It is!" she cried. "I just can't stand it."

Ginger was not yet aware of her potential inner resources. She could learn to handle this situation just like she had learned to walk and talk. However, she was going to need some support to take on this challenge. Developing her own autonomy was going to become Ginger's love song to Bud.

AUTONOMY—WHAT IS IT?

Autonomy is the ability to function independently whenever necessary. In marriage it means enjoying the love and support of your mate when it is available, but being able to love and support yourself when he or she is not available. The strongest marriages are those where a husband and wife come together to give of themselves to each other. Both receive something from the other because both have a "full cup" to share.

However, in many marriages either one or both parties are overly dependent upon the other for nurture. When two people approach each other wanting their empty cups filled by their mate, neither is going to be satisfied. The dependent person in such a situation tends to blame the other when nurturing is not forthcoming. The autonomous person will manage until he or she can find other constructive ways for self-nurture.

This is not to say that autonomy means the kind of individualism where one functions solely to meet one's own needs. Being able to stand alone when necessary does not mean we can never be intimate or vulnerable. An autonomous person does not refuse help when it's needed. An autonomous person is independent enough to *choose* how and when to become involved with others.

When does autonomy become pride? George is a man who does not like to lean on anybody for anything. He once gave himself a hernia lifting something too heavy by himself rather than asking for help. This is pride, not autonomy. To be autonomous means to accept personal responsibility for identifying and satisfying our own personal needs, which may well involve the help of other people. We don't blame our mate for not giving us what we want; we look for constructive alternatives.

Autonomy requires self-representation, not dependency upon another person to think and speak on one's behalf. It is the capacity for independent functioning.

We become autonomous when we have individuated from our parents so that we do not project onto our mate those expectations that we learned to anticipate from our parents. Autonomy in marriage is the capacity to enjoy our husband's or wife's personality and characteristics without placing the person under unrealistic expectations to be what we want them to be.

Can a Christian be autonomous? Some people think that, to promote autonomy, they need to reject the Christian idea that we should be dependent upon God for all things. But functioning independently does not mean we should function independent of God. As Christians we know that it is God who gives us our life and breath. Apart from God we are nothing. It is God in whom "we live and move and have our being" (Acts 17:28). God in us gives our lives meaning and power. We are constantly dependent upon God.

We all have moments when we are less stable and need extra help. Becoming ill or unemployed or discouraged during some crisis causes us to need to lean on God and others for support. One of the joys of marriage is that a husband and wife can be available to each other for support when needed. However, some people lean on others too much. Those who are emotionally dependent expect others to take care of them because they do not know how to take care of themselves.

Ginger had never been in a position where she needed to act autonomously. Bud had been a strong source of support for her ever since she moved out of her parents' home. Their present situation was a more radical shift than she had ever had to face. Although she was capable of learning how to be more autonomous, she had never realized that this was a necessary part of life. Now she was frightened at the sudden changes required of her. This challenging situation represented an opportunity for her to grow from dependency to autonomy.

Dependent spouses seek closeness for their own comfort and reassurance rather than for mutual concern. They rely upon routine roles for "a track to run on." They organize themselves around others with stronger identities for their own self-definition. Instead of operating out of a strong sense of their own inner being, they *react* to others. They don't act on their own. They feel lost by themselves when there is no one to whom they can react.

THE SIGNIFICANCE OF AUTONOMY

Autonomy is an important ingredient in a healthy marriage.

Our mate may not always be available to support us when we need it. Suppose our mate is ill, or out of town, or depressed, or struggling with major issues of life, needing support as much as we do. This is when a husband and wife especially need to be autonomous. Our personal autonomy allows us to be self-confident when we are left alone with our unresolved needs.

Ginger was noticeably self-conscious returning to my office with Bud. Her ambivalence about herself was apparent in her face as she began to speak.

"I am so confused. I don't know what is right anymore. I just know that I am mad about Bud's job coming between us and I'm getting the feeling that I shouldn't be. Is that so bad? Am I wrong to love my husband so much that I want to be with him?" she queried.

Ginger wasn't yet able to see that her desire to have Bud home rather than away on business was based on her dependency needs rather than on her caring about Bud's needs. She was open to what I had to say, however, and made a giant step in coming to grips with this problem.

"I didn't realize I was being so selfish, Bud. I hope you'll forgive me!" she cried. "It's just that I'm so scared. I guess I'll just have to face it!"

Bud responded sensitively. "I'm sorry this has been so hard for you, honey. I want to help in any way I can, but we can't afford for me to leave my job. I hope you can understand."

Autonomy vs. codependence. Unlike Bud, some people enjoy the feeling of importance they get when their mate depends heavily upon them. They are known as codependents because they are dependent upon their partner's dependency. They do things to encourage their spouse's continued dependent behavior. Codependents find their identity by attaching to others rather than discovering themselves and learning how to meet their own needs.

Fortunately for Ginger, Bud is not codependent. He is autonomous enough to believe in his own love for Ginger and can see the insecurity that she is experiencing. He listens to her, holds her, reassures her of his love, and encourages her to talk about her feelings. Without defending himself or giving her a lot of advice that she isn't ready to hear, he lets her talk about her fears and her loneliness and encourages her to continue with counseling. This is Bud's love song to Ginger.

Ginger is beginning to realize that there are more things she needs to do for herself. She has met some women friends at church whose company she enjoys on a regular basis. She is also working part-time as a sales person at a bakery. In general she is learning to respond to her own needs without expecting someone else to do things for her that she can do for herself.

Strength to spare. Our personal autonomy contributes to our own well-being. But autonomy is also important to our marriage because it enables us to bring more to that relationship. As autonomous individuals, we have more to share.

An autonomous person has more of a self to reveal to his or her mate. An autonomous person also is able to be emotionally supportive in times of pain for the other person. We stand beside our spouse in his or her hard times because that is the loving thing to do. The mutual sharing of each other's concerns is what brings people closer together and creates intimacy in a relationship.

AUTONOMY OR CONTROL

A person can look autonomous on the surface, however, and still be dependent. When Mike and Sally appeared in my office the first time, I could feel the tension between them. Sally felt that Mike was overcontrolling of her and the children. He would yell at the children for minor infractions and be overcritical if Sally didn't do things the way he thought they should be done.

Mike seemed secure in his dominant position, but he was actually overcompensating for his feelings of inadequacy. His own insecurities made him seek control of others to give him the illusory reassurance that he was important and competent. Mike was not autonomous or capable of seeing himself objectively. He was very dependent upon his family for love. Unfortunately, he didn't believe himself to be lovable so he tried to make himself feel loved by getting his way all the time.

Mike's family did love him, but he constantly undermined it with criticism and unsolicited advice. When Sally would react negatively to this, he would blame her for not loving him. Mike was emotionally dependent but masked it with his dominant behavior. He was strong in his reactions to others, but he was not emotionally autonomous.

Our autonomy provides stability in relationships. Because autonomy is not overly possessive or dependent, both parties feel secure enough in themselves not to make demands upon each other. This minimizes fighting and discord and puts marital commitment on a stronger footing.

It takes two autonomous people to make a healthy relationship. To alternate between passion and intimacy requires two people to be strong enough in themselves to be vulnerable about their need for closeness, yet willing to be apart so that their passion can build again.

DEVELOPING AUTONOMY

If autonomy is so important to having an intimate relationship, we need to know how to develop it in our own personal lives. Consider these three aspects of autonomy to evaluate yourself:

1. Independent thinking. In order to be able to *function* independently, it is important for us to be able to *think* independently. It is easy to accept traditional values because so many other people accept them. This may give us acceptance by our parents and peer groups. However, to develop independent thinking, we need to process these traditional values for ourselves. We need to make decisions about what we believe because *we* have chosen to believe them, and not just because our parents, pastors, professors, or counselors have told us we should. Independent thinking is difficult and sometimes frightening for those who are not in the habit of trusting their own thought processes.

Betty was never encouraged as a child to think for herself. When she first came to me for counseling she said, "I am a social chameleon. What I think depends upon who I am with at the moment. I feel like I don't have any personality or opinions of my own on anything. My views are constantly changing because everybody seems to make sense. Just when I make up my mind about something, somebody else comes along and changes it."

This is a very painful place in which to be. It makes one feel lost, inadequate, defective, and of little worth. Unfortunately, it is common.

Consider Bud and Ginger again. Bud is an independent thinker. He was given more opportunity to make his own decisions as a child than was Ginger. He was never shamed or humiliated for making a bad decision even though he got himself into trouble occasionally. Because Bud has had a lot of encouragement and practice at thinking for himself, he is able to feel confident in expressing his viewpoint to others. Also, he can bring more to his marriage because he interacts thoughtfully with his world outside of his marriage. He has opinions and feelings about his experiences each day that make for interesting conversation at night.

Some of us are reluctant to think for ourselves because we fear being rejected for thinking differently. This oversensitivity to rejection is the product of our needing approval from others because we do not know how to approve of ourselves. Yet if we could learn to risk thinking and expressing our beliefs, we might eventually find support for our views. Then we would eventually begin to need that support less.

We need to decide *what* we believe, our own personal philosophy of life. I cannot remember ever not being a Christian. However, I am sure that my earliest belief was due to my childhood training rather than my thinking for myself. As I continued to grow intellectually, I began to realize that I needed to have my own reasons for being a Christian. I learned to examine my life from a biblical viewpoint and I made some important decisions.

Our Christian faith gives us a solid basis for living. However we need to claim it for ourselves because we have found our own faith in Christ and not because somebody has told us what to believe. The decision to believe in Jesus Christ must be our own decision. Nobody else can make that decision for us. This is part of being autonomous.

I remain a Christian because, as I look over my personal history, I can see how God has been working in my life to bring me closer to himself and to others. I believe God's priority is relationships. He first wants me to trust him, obey him, and be available to him for his creative purposes. As I do this, I affirm my relationship with him. He affirms his relationship with me as he opens and closes doors in my life, as he loves me through other people, and as he sustains me in the face of serious challenges. I believe that my Creator is actively involved in my life to the degree that I am open and receptive to him.

This belief is personal to me. Some believers will vary from this point of view, but the point here is that whatever you believe, it needs to be your own considered belief.

2. Dealing with our needs. Having needs is a normal part of life. A need is a tension which seeks resolution. When we are hungry, we eat to resolve the tension of our hunger. When we are fatigued, we rest. When we are lonely, we seek out a friend. When we feel confined, we seek freedom.

The rhythm of life is tension/resolution, need-awareness/ need-fulfillment. Therefore it is important for us to identify our physical, emotional, and spiritual needs in order to act toward their resolution. God gave us these tensions to motivate us into creative activity.

We have already discussed that autonomy means accepting responsibility for identifying our own personal needs and doing our best to satisfy them in constructive ways. Unfortunately some of us have gotten discouraged about having our needs satisfied. This often leads us to rationalize that we don't have any needs.

At first glance, it might sound wonderful to be married to someone like this. After all, he or she won't be making any demands on us. However, sooner or later we start to realize that our spouse doesn't need *us* either. What we have to give isn't valued or appreciated by someone who seems to have no needs.

Denying the existence of our needs may sound very autonomous, but autonomy does not mean denial of our needs. Healthy autonomy includes the willingness to deal with our own frustration when our needs are not satisfied. When we are thirsty we don't pretend we are not just because there is no water available. Instead, we respond to the need by resolving it with a satisfying drink of water as soon as we are able.

Many of us reject our emotional needs because we don't like the vulnerable feeling of wanting something we may not be able to have. However, to deny awareness of our own needs is an ineffective attempt to escape the discomfort of unfulfillment. Of course we all have needs, but not all of us are able to clearly identify them. As autonomous individuals, we will learn to identify and accept our own needs and seek responsible ways to satisfy them. This is another way to sing the love song of autonomy.

Joe was feeling lethargic and dissatisfied with life one day. So he sat down in a quiet place and began thinking about his life. He realized that this feeling began two days ago, so he asked himself what was going on in his life two days ago. Eventually he remembered that he had had a busy day which had included an unpleasant confrontation with someone at work. But the day was so busy that Joe didn't have time to reflect upon the experience and come to any resolution about it in his mind. The more it slipped out of his consciousness, the more depressed he became. Once he remembered what had happened, he could review the incident in his mind and he could come to peace with it. Joe had taken personal responsibility for dealing with his need to resolve his mood. Joe was acting autonomously. He might have been able to accomplish the same thing by talking to his wife. But some people are better facilitators than others, and some people would just rather think things out first before they share them.

3. Dealing with emotional pain. Part of the autonomous love song is learning to manage our own emotional pain, which is a particular category of our personal needs. If we fail to do this, we often end up acting in an unloving way toward others. For example, if our mate says something that hurts our feelings, unless we know how to deal with our own pain, we may retaliate or say something we regret.

Many of us have the notion that we should be able to get through life without feeling hurt. We resent pain and will seek to avoid it at any cost. However, avoiding pain is ultimately more costly since avoidance prevents resolution and prolongs the suffering. The only way for emotional hurts to heal is for us to face them squarely and experience our feelings until our mind and body gradually feel some resolve. When we lose someone important to us through death, it is normal to grieve. The only real healing comes from mourning our loss. When our inner feelings are clearly focused on what we have lost, we gradually work our way through the emotional pain. Unfortunately, many of us try to circumvent this by pretending we do not hurt. This denial or repression of painful feelings prevents emotional healing and creates undesirable symptoms.

It is not our nature to put up with pain if there is any way to avoid it. But we think we are avoiding pain when we are not. Pretending that things don't bother us or becoming involved in distracting activities does not remove the pain. These activities simply prolong it by not allowing our mind to process and dissipate the pain through necessary, conscious experience.

Autonomous people face and deal with whatever emotional pain is present. They accept their need for comfort and support from others, but they also know how to cry alone. Without this capacity to face one's own pain, a person may become an unnecessary burden on his or her mate. It is not unthinkable for one spouse to comfort and be with the other in their pain. But if the hurting person gives the impression that he or she can never cope alone, then the comforting spouse feels a heavy responsibility to keep the other emotionally stable. This can create a parent-child type of relationship which makes the comforting spouse afraid of ever leaning on the less stable spouse for occasional support. Well-developed autonomy permits both partners in a marriage to seek comfort when it is available, but it allows them to comfort themselves when support from their mate may not be available.

There are two essential ingredients that we need in our lives if we are to be able to manage our own emotional hurts. The first is the occasional experience of pain itself. If we don't experience pain, how can we learn to cope with it? We don't go looking for hurtful experiences, but we do need them in our lives occasionally in order to learn to cope with major painful experiences we may face down the line. It is a developmental process we all need to grow through.

Barbara looked stunned when I first saw her in my office. Until recently, she had led a fairy tale life. Now, in midlife, everything had fallen apart. Her husband had left her for another woman. She was so shaken she couldn't keep her job. Then one of her children committed suicide. She had no experience in dealing with disappointments or tragedies prior to this. Barbara needed a lot of support to help her through this experience. She had to do some fast growing to cope with it all.

It is best to be open to life's realities as they happen to us. Parents who protect children from disappointments and hurts mean well, but only make it more difficult for them to adjust in later life.

The second essential ingredient in learning to cope with emotional pain is the experience of a supportive, trustworthy, reassuring person who can encourage us as we experience our hurt without trying to take away our pain. This may seem obvious to some, but I am constantly meeting people in my office who get so anxious when their spouse hurts that they try to take away their emotional pain. On the surface it may seem like a kind and loving thing to do, but in reality it is not helpful.

Bud does not like to see Ginger hurting, but he knows that the only way for her to grow into autonomy is to feel the pain of her aloneness so that she can develop her coping ability. He loves her enough to hurt with her instead of "fixing" her pain so that *he* can be more comfortable. This is his love song to Ginger. If he distracts her from her pain, it will only prevent her from growing.

The only way to deal with pain is to experience it until we one day realize that it doesn't intimidate us as much as it once did. Having a supportive person in our lives is important to help us reach this point. A patient and understanding person can help us gain the confidence we need to face pain in the future.

Overprotection vs. underprotection. Not all of us have experienced the right mix of emotional pain in a context of loving support. On the one hand, some of us were *over*protected children who experienced lots of security and encouragement, but not much pain on which to practice developing our coping skills.

On the other hand, some of us were *under*protected children who were rejected and often ignored or abused. We experienced lots of pain with which to practice coping, but not enough loving support to encourage the development of constructive coping skills. We lack confidence in coping with pain because we learned to rely upon suppression, denial, or avoidance to survive.

The pain seemed too overwhelming to face alone. Therefore we learned to rely solely on our respective defense mechanisms for coping. It never occurred to us that there might be supportive and loving people in this world. This attitude and experience sets us up for the impulsive move toward quick comforts. Addiction to alcohol, drugs, sex, or food are examples of efforts to comfort ourselves when we don't believe we qualify for a loving relationship. Addictions are a counterfeit solution to a legitimate need.

It is interesting to notice some implications for marriage here. A husband and wife who were both properly supported as children and learned to deal with their pain are going to have the most satisfying marriage of all. They are more self-confident and more secure in themselves both as individuals and as a couple. When one steps on the other's toes, they talk about it, forgive, and get on with their lives. Most of us, however, come to marriage with some level of imbalance.

Bill and Linda were both *under*protected as children. They are both independent and self-reliant. The bad news is that neither feels important to the other, and they don't know how to give to each other emotionally. This couple's intimate moments together are few and brief. They have a lot of autonomy but are afraid of intimacy. As long as their passionate desire can be satisfied occasionally, they can manage. However, they need to work at singing a love song of trust and openness to each other to keep their relationship at its best.

Dale and Virginia were both *over*protected as children. They tend to lean on each other a lot. They are intimate with each other, but their relationship lacks spark because they relate more out of their insecurity than their confidence. They have little sense of their own identity, they both hate being alone, they have developed few capacities for self-nurture, and they lack self-confidence. Their relationship is limited, but both are too dependent to do anything about it. These people need to sing a love song of autonomy and take more responsibility for their own lives so that they have more to bring to their marriage.

Brent was an *over*protected child and Judy was an *under*protected child. Brent wants more intimacy than Judy. When Brent moves closer and Judy moves away, he feels frustrated and she feels guilty. This situation requires Brent to sing a love song of autonomy and Judy to sing a love song of intimacy. They both must talk about their respective needs, asking for what they want, and giving whatever they are able.

In some cases, one partner comes from a background of having been over- or underprotected, while other person was properly supported as a child. The one who was properly supported as a child can bring stability to a marriage and improve its chances for harmony. The most difficult marriage adjustments occur when both husband and wife have had upbringings lacking in one or more of the ways we have described.

Managing our own emotional pain provides stability in our relationship. Through loving forgiveness and personal pain tolerance, we minimize emotional overreaction, rejection, fighting, and discord. We set an example for our children and for each other as we practice the art of relational healing.

LEARNING TO COPE

Since it is so important for us to be able to manage our own hurts, how can we learn to do this? How can we better sing our love song of autonomy by developing stronger emotional coping resources?

1. Believe that God will sustain us. Believe that God expects us to trust him when we hurt. First Corinthians 10:13 tells us that God will not let us be pushed beyond our limits. In 2 Corinthians 12 we read of Paul's thorn in the flesh and how God's grace was sufficient to sustain Paul.

2. Look for the meaning in our pain. Suffering is more bearable when it has a purpose. A missionary couple returned home when John developed tuberculosis. Mary had to redefine her ministry in terms of caring for her husband. Although she was disappointed in having to leave their work behind, she found meaning in loving John in his illness. She accommodated herself to her new life out of love for John as God helped her recognize another form of ministry.

We do not always know the purpose of our suffering. Sometimes we must simply trust God that there is a purpose. When we can do this, it is our love song to God.

3. Pray for our mate when he or she has hurt us. Have you ever tried to get revenge against someone while simultaneously praying for that person? It isn't possible to do both at once. Prayer puts us in touch with God, our greatest resource for loving, forgiving, and coping with pain.

4. Meditate upon Scripture when we are alone and hurting. Passages such as Romans 8, Philippians 3, and many of the Psalms are helpful during these times. As we practice the presence of God in our lives through time spent in prayer and meditation upon the Scriptures, we can renew our spirit and find motivation and power to love.

5. Build our own supportive network. I never wake up from a night's sleep without being grateful to God for my wife. However as much as we love each other, we recognize that it is unrealistic for us to meet all of each other's needs. When we first moved to Orange County in 1981, we didn't know anybody. But little by little we came to make new friends as a couple and as individuals. We get something a little different from everyone.

Hopefully they get something they need from us.

I can tell when Arleen has just been with some of her women friends. She seems lifted up, more self-confident, and has more to talk about. Similarly, when I have been with my men friends, I have received a lift from being able to exchange thoughts, feelings, and experiences with them. I value my time spent with them. Whether we are laughing together or crying together, there is a unity of spirit and acceptance that energizes me so that I have more to give to my wife.

Some of us find this threatening. We want to be the center of our mate's life and we may become jealous if anyone else becomes important to our mate. However, having a supportive network in our life only enriches our marriage as long as we are also doing everything we can to be intimate with our mate.

Accepting personal responsibility for our own personal network of support demonstrates a healthy autonomy within our marriage. This is the beginning of intimacy. Our level of true intimacy cannot exceed our level of autonomy. It's like two sides of the same coin: whatever size the coin, one side is never larger than the other.

We have been discussing ways to develop our own autonomy. This is done partially through independent thinking, managing our own personal needs, and learning to deal with emotional pain. Another way to develop autonomy in ourselves is to practice forgiveness.

LEARNING TO FORGIVE

An important reason for facing our emotional pain is so that we can forgive our mate and be reconciled to him or her. Forgiveness releases others from responsibility for the pain they have caused us. It doesn't matter if the offending party wants to be forgiven. It is still a loving act which strengthens our relationship with God. It also releases us from bitterness, allowing us to move ahead with our lives without a lot of unresolved emotional baggage. Forgiveness requires willingness to accept the pain of another's hurtful behavior toward us. We cannot forgive unless we are able to accept our pain.

In Colossians 3:13 we read, "Bear with each other and forgive whatever grievances you may have against one another. Forgive as the Lord forgave you." In Mark 11:25 we find, "When you [pray], if you hold anything against anyone, forgive him, so that your Father in heaven may forgive you your sins."

The secret to forgiveness is the willingness to suffer and absorb the pain that has been inflicted upon us by another. This means accepting the event, how it hurts, and expressing the pain by crying, praying, and sharing it with a trusted and understanding friend.

Jesus was a man of sorrows, acquainted with grief. He knows about suffering. He suffers with every sin that separates us from God. Knowing this can encourage us as we participate in the fellowship of his sufferings. We can tell him about our pain; he can be trusted above all human friends.

Resentment results when we refuse to face emotional pain. Lucille came to my office because she couldn't get past her resentment at Tom for divorcing her. Lucille had never been allowed to be weak in her family. As the oldest child, she grew up taking care of her brother, sister, and even her parents, all at her own emotional expense. She did this with her husband Tom as wellv and she was angry that all of her hard work and self-sacrifice only resulted in rejection.

I listened to Lucille's anger for a while. Then I said, "Lucille, I hear a lot of anger, but I think I hear something else behind it. Aren't you pretty hurt by this whole experience?"

"No, I'm angry at what Tom has done to me. Don't I have a right to be angry?" she asked sternly.

"Of course you do, Lucille, but you have been angry a long time now. I think it is time to start allowing yourself to feel your pain. Don't you think you are angry because your husband has hurt you?" She started to cry.

"I was never allowed to hurt before," she stammered.

"Your pain," I said, "is your primary feeling and you won't get past your anger until you can 'own' your pain." She didn't realize how much she had been resisting feeling her pain.

When Lucille accepted her right to feel pain for herself, she cried intensely. The more she allowed herself to feel her pain, the less angry she had to be to defend against it. Because she was accepting her pain, her anger began to diminish and she could start forgiving Tom.

This is what Lucille needs to do internally. But how does she act toward Tom from this point? It depends upon whether or not Tom wants forgiveness. If he does, she has not truly forgiven him until she can tell him so. How this is done depends upon circumstances. I recommend that she forgives him (in order of preference) face to face, on the phone, or in a letter. Face to face contact makes forgiveness more powerful, although there may be obstacles, such as geographical distance that makes this impractical .

If Tom does not care about being forgiven, then the forgiveness may or may not be declared. But Lucille still needs to forgive him so that she can be free of guilt for closing the door to possible reconciliation. God wants all relationships to be reconciled to him and to each other. Obviously this requires both sides to cooperate: one forgives and the other humbly accepts it. But this is not always the case.

Sometimes the one we need to forgive is dead. This does not close the door on forgiveness, however. Until we forgive everyone who has offended us, dead or alive, the door is not completely closed on this issue. It may be helpful to speak to the one who has died in our imagination and say the forgiving things we have to say. Writing a letter may be helpful in terms of organizing your thoughts. Rereading it can also be helpful in bringing closure to your relationship.

Forgiving a person who does not want forgiveness is problematic for some who need to feel validated by acceptance of their forgiving effort. However, acceptance should not be the criteria for reaching out in the first place. We forgive because God tells us to. It opens the door for possible reconciliation, reduces our own psychological tension, and enhances our spiritual consciousness of God. As we receive God's forgiveness for our own transgressions, we must be willing to convey God's grace by forgiving others. This is actually a cause to rejoice that God can live through us as we are available to him to be witnesses to his love and grace.

As we seek to forgive, we must remember that forgiving is both an attitude and a behavior. It is not a feeling although there are strong feelings involved. We may feel vulnerable, wounded, hurt, sad, or humiliated. But regardless of what we feel or how long we feel it, forgiveness is ultimately a behavior. Just because you feel bad for days or weeks, doesn't mean you haven't forgiven. You still need recovery time for yourself. The way you know you have forgiven is that you no longer act critical or resentful but kind, positive, and open to relating on some level.

The ability to forgive is a major indicator of our emotional autonomy. How autonomous are you? Do you think for yourself? Do you accept responsibility for your own needs? Can you cope with emotional pain? Can you forgive rather than hold a grudge?

Arleen and I never retire at night without sharing our experiences of the day and our feelings toward each other. We have found nurturance from a variety of resources and we come together to share from our "full cup." If we want to have something to give our mate, we must be autonomous in filling our own cup so that we can give it away to our mate and to others.

One way we sing our love song is to be autonomous and responsible for our own attitudes, feelings, needs, and behavior. This brings stability and richness to our marriage, and also enhances our ability to alternate between passion and intimacy. One important way we develop autonomy is by learning to forgive. This involves trusting God to sustain us through our own personal pain. When we have developed autonomy in our own personal life, we have laid a strong foundation for finding true intimacy in our marriage relationship.

With an understanding of autonomy as the foundation of intimacy, let us look more closely at the process of developing intimacy. I call it learning to sing the love song of self-disclosure and the love song of acceptance.

CHAPTER SIX

The Revealing Love Song

Jerry was a police officer who came to counseling at the request of his wife. Lois had always thought being married to a policeman would be great. It would be like having a built-in security system. This appealed to her a great deal. However, over their fifteen-year marriage, she began to realize that she didn't really feel secure at all. Jerry was a likeable person with a good sense of humor. He seemed to have his act together pretty well and people were always coming to him for advice. But now Lois had dragged him into my office for some marriage counseling.

"You never tell me what's going on," Lois cried. "You won't let me be part of this marriage! You make decisions without me. When you are hurting over something at work, I am the last to know. You don't tell me anything until it is ancient history. I'm feeling more and more anxious each day because I seem to know less and less about what's going on with you. Does everything in your life have to be a secret? How can I relax when you never tell me what you are thinking?"

Jerry reacted. "I don't want to trouble you with all of my problems. I want to protect you from all the hassles I face every day. I wish you could appreciate that."

"But you didn't even tell me *that* until just now!" Lois

rebutted. "This kind of protection I don't need."

Although Jerry may have intended to "protect" Lois from his "problems," he in effect was creating a bigger burden for her without realizing it. It was the burden of isolation, of his not sharing his concerns with her so that she could be intimately involved with him.

Jerry and Lois are not alone. This is a common misunderstanding. Many individuals, male and female, do not think they should be too open with their mate. Although they say they are being protective of their mate, they are more often than not trying to protect themselves from having to deal with their mate's reaction. Fear that we can't work it out together often leads us into handling things on our own. This attitude and behavior, however, is not conducive to a healthy marriage. It might seem that Jerry is being autonomous by protecting Lois from his concerns. But he is actually shutting her out of his personal life. Autonomy is the ability to stand alone when your mate is not available to support you. But Lois wants to support Jerry. She wants to feel important to him.

For two people to love one another and care about their respective needs, each one has to know a lot about the other. We can presume a few things about our mate just by observation over a period of time, but we can't really know his or her feelings, beliefs, or desires—who this person really is—unless we are told directly. And we have to reciprocate. Only by mutual sharing of ourselves can we ever hope to be close.

Intimate self-disclosure in marriage is the process of revealing our innermost private thoughts and feelings to our mate. This does not mean that we cannot keep some things private. However, the more we can share with our spouse, the greater the intimacy level will be.

LEVELS OF SELF-DISCLOSURE

Because marital intimacy is a husband and wife knowing personal details of each other's lives, it is important for us to reveal these details to one another, voluntarily. Self-disclosure gives our mate an opportunity to know who we are at that moment. This equips our spouse to relate to us with sensitivity and loving care.

To reveal ourselves means to divulge or entrust to our mate our innermost private thoughts and feelings. This involves past, present, and future aspects of our lives as well as feelings such as joy, sadness, anger, and fear. Personal self-disclosure is another way we sing our love song to our mate.

There is a kind of communication that is not self-disclosing at all. I call it the "news, weather, and sports" kind of dialogue. We need this communication of facts to function in our day-to-day world. This impersonal kind of relating is helpful in taking care of our necessary business. However it reveals little of ourselves and does nothing to produce intimacy.

"The radio said it will be colder tomorrow."

"There may be a new breakthrough in cancer research."

"The Dodgers are on a winning streak."

Facts like these are impersonal. Disclosing personal facts about ourselves, however, is the first real level of intimacy. Examples of *personal* facts are:

"The doctor removed a mole from my arm today."

"I was given a good evaluation at work today."

"That meal we ate out gave me indigestion."

Personal facts are important to initiating and establishing intimacy. But they are the least intimate level of sharing.

The second level of intimacy is achieved by sharing *feelings* as well as facts. Let us look at the previous examples in terms of this deeper level of communication:

"I was *relieved* to have the doctor tell me my mole was benign."

"I was so *excited* about my evaluation at work today!"

"I am so *annoyed* at that restaurant! I *hate* paying them to give me indigestion."

Many of us think we are sharing feelings just because we preface our facts with phrases such as "I feel like" or "I feel that." For example, "I *feel like* we should try again," or "I *feel that* we can do it" are expressions of belief, but not of feeling. Although beliefs are valid ways of disclosing ourselves, sharing feelings is more personal than sharing opinions or beliefs.

Here are some more examples of feeling words.

"I am *eager* for us to try again."

"I was *sad* that you seemed to be giving up."

"I am *pleased* that you stuck with it."

"I am *angry* at myself for not trying harder."

"I feel *guilty* not supporting you more."

Feelings and emotions increase the level of personal self-disclosure between people. Yet there is still another level which is the most personal and intimate of all.

It is sharing how we feel about the person to whom we are speaking.

"I *appreciate* you for suggesting I see a doctor."

"I *resent* your crack about my job evaluation."

"I *enjoyed* being with you at dinner even though the food was terrible."

It is one thing to share how we feel about something outside of our relationship, but it is much more intimate to share with our spouse how we feel toward him or her. This is one of the best ways there is to sing a love song. Whether it is positive or negative, it is revealing of our innermost feelings toward our mate.

ARE YOU A REVEALER OR A CONCEALER?

Are you a "Revealer" or a "Concealer"? Do you make it possible for your mate to know you from the inside out? Or do you hide your thoughts, needs, feelings, and experiences?

What can we reveal? I often hear clients in my office say they have run out of things to talk about. What do intimate couples talk about besides facts like news, weather, and sports?

1. Present feelings. Sharing our feelings in the present moment is one way to share something meaningful. Lois wanted to know more of what Jerry was thinking and feeling. He said he didn't want to burden her with his problems. However, as it turned out, the truth was that he felt too vulnerable opening up to her. The result was that Lois felt closed out and alone. She didn't know how to give to Jerry because he never revealed any needs or concerns.

Jerry never felt safe sharing his feelings with anybody. He had been hurt in the past and learned to protect himself. He learned so well that he has little conscious awareness of his feelings anymore. Now he lives a life of logical problem-solving in a job that requires discipline, self-control, and risk of his own physical safety, with a minimum of emotional response. Jerry didn't realize how important it was to Lois for him to share his struggles until she got angry about it.

If angry feelings are not expressed, these feelings can build up within us and create emotional or physiological problems. This can result in resentment, depression, displaced hostility, headaches, ulcers, or gastrointestinal problems.

A mentally healthy person is one who knows what he or she is feeling and to what those feelings are connected. However, if it is too threatening to admit to ourselves that we are either angry, frightened, or hurt, then our specific feelings become generalized into displaced hostility, anxiety, or depression. Many people are frightened by their feelings. Not everyone has been taught how to cope with and express their feelings in healthy, constructive ways. If we are afraid to reveal our anger to the person with whom we are angry, we may displace our anger onto a safer person, even if they don't deserve it. It's the old "kick the dog" syndrome. Or if we try to avoid thinking about something that frightens us, we may repress our fear and become anxious about everything in general.

Many people are not tuned in to their own feelings, either because they were never encouraged to be, or because their feelings are not comfortable to think about. Others know what they are feeling but, like Jerry, choose not to reveal them. This undermines intimacy. If we expect to be close to someone, we need to share our feelings in the present moment.

Sharing feelings is important if our mate is to know us intimately. Yet anger seems to be a feeling that spoils intimacy because of how it is revealed.

Anger is a strong feeling of displeasure. We cannot always help what we feel in the immediate moment, but we must be accountable for how we express our feelings. How should anger be handled best in a marriage in order to promote intimacy?

If we are angry toward our mate for something, intimacy would require that we reveal that feeling to our spouse. The problem is that most of us have not had constructive role models for expressing anger. Yelling, using foul language or degrading terms, or throwing things are simply not appropriate ways to express anger. They provoke the other person to withdraw or fight back. It is an understatement to point out that this does not encourage intimacy! Responsible communication that gets the message across in a firm but kind way, however, enhances intimacy.

Although there are certain schools of thought that would encourage these ventilating approaches as healthy, the Bible says "in your anger do not sin" (Eph 4:26). This means to be aware of our feelings but not act it out in a destructive manner. We can learn to control our actions, to express even the strongest feelings in a constructive manner. For example, we can say, "I don't like what you are doing and I want you to stop." The words can communicate without demeaning the listener.

Some psychologists consider this type of statement as lacking in authenticity unless we are dramatically showing how emotionally stirred up we are. Carol Tavris has written *Anger: The Misunderstood Emotion*,[1] which is an excellent book championing the opposite point of view, the responsible approach to expressing anger.

Much of anger is emotional dependency. We get upset if our mate doesn't sing the love song we want to hear. We assume our spouse doesn't really love us if he or she doesn't perform the way that makes us comfortable. Some of us get our feelings hurt easily because we rely on our mate to make us happy. Anger based upon this perspective is immature. We will never be happy until we can draw our resources from God as well as from our mate. It is wonderful how God gives us so much nurturance through our mate. God wants us to enjoy our mate. But our stability and true worth comes from God, not our mate.

Expressing our present feelings is an important way to reveal ourselves to our mate. But there are other things to reveal as well.

2. Sharing our personal history. Revealing our past is usually done more in the earlier stages of a relationship. But in some cases, I find that couples are slow to reveal their past even after they have been married for years. Learning about each other's past is helpful in understanding what experiences have helped shape us into the persons that we are.

For example, knowing that Darlene was an abused child is an intimate detail that enables Dave to be more sensitive to the emotional scars that she carries from her past. Realizing how she was put down and humiliated, much of her childhood helps Dave understand her shyness and fears, enabling him to be more sympathetic and loving.

Sharing our personal history is invaluable in promoting intimacy. Peter was afraid to tell his wife Margie about his background. Peter had served a brief jail term prior to meeting her. He was afraid Margie might not marry him if she knew. Even though he had had a clean record for the past few years, Peter was afraid to risk losing her. By concealing this fact from her, he was setting her up for great distrust should she ever find out. She might wonder what else he hadn't told her. Although we can understand Peter's feelings, it is also true that anyone who could not accept him as he was did not show much promise as a good mate.

3. Revealing hopes and dreams. Sharing our hopes, dreams, and aspirations is another way to reveal ourselves. Knowing what is important to each other promotes familiarity and intimacy. It also enables our spouse to support us in our dreams. Sometimes our dreams are long-term goals that may have little chance of ever coming to pass. In other cases they may be more short-term and realistic. But regardless of their potential for achievement, sharing our goals with one another helps both to feel connected to each other.

One of my secret ambitions in life was to sing with a live orchestra. Two significant factors kept interfering with my dream: my shyness, and my lack of talent. I wanted to major in music at Westmont College, so I had to take all kinds of tests to measure my musical aptitude. The professor of music who counseled me looked at my test results and asked me if I had considered any other majors. With that bit of encouragement, I decided to just take a class in choral conducting, which I passed by the skin of my teeth.

I still had my dream to sing with an orchestra, however. One day, years later, I got my chance. I auditioned for a part in "Fiddler on the Roof" at Glendale College. They told me the main roles were already filled, unless my name was Mario Lanza. But if I wanted to be one of the "townspeople," I could be in their production. Well, I accepted. Somehow I got a one-line part and when they realized I could be heard in the back of the auditorium, I ended up with about eight one-liners. The real joy, however, came when I was chosen as one of six to sing a song with the orchestra.

You see music is a part of who I am, and it is important to me for my wife to know that about me. Even though I feel foolish and vulnerable talking about it, this sharing of hopes and dreams is a part of being intimate.

Ted wanted to be a medical missionary, as did his wife Joan. They shared a dream. Even though Ted started to go blind and their dream could not be realized, they had shared something together—the joy of their dream as well as the disappointment and rearrangement of their plans. They mutually supported one another as they shared their love song of intimacy together.

4. Revealing personal needs. Spouses often differ in their concept of needs. Some feel free about admitting their need for comfort, support, and time together. Others feel awkward asking for anything. Still others aren't even aware of their needs. Sharing our needs is another way of becoming intimate as well as an avenue for having those needs satisfied.

Since many people are not accustomed to reflecting upon their own emotional needs, a few examples may be in order. Most of us have a need to be loved and appreciated. We want to feel significant to others. In order to feel satisfied with life, we seek comfort from the stresses of life. We want the security of knowing our relationships are stable. We need people to understand our feelings and to care about us. We need time for solitude as well as time to socialize. We need to express our own creativity. We need to feel confident in our abilities and in our lovability. We need friends, not just acquaintances. We need recreation and play.

Needs vary from person to person as well as from time to time. Because of this, it is appropriate to share our needs with one another in order that we can be known. This is our love song to our partner—as long as it doesn't come across as a demand.

Clients have said to me, "I have tried sharing my needs with my spouse, but it doesn't work!" What they really mean is that they expect to be given exactly what they have requested. We need to remind ourselves that an autonomous person asks for what is desired, but does not seek to control or demand.

Love cannot be controlled or demanded, only given and received. We must reveal our needs, accepting whatever response we get. It is hard for many of us to reveal a need knowing it may not be met. But love for our spouse should be unconditional acceptance of that person, regardless of his or her response to us. Love isn't a matter of merely "liking"; it is a behavior that has both positive and negative feelings connected to it.

In other words, our spouse will never be able to sing every note of every love song we want to hear. Our spouse will sing his or her own love song, leaving out some of our favorite notes and including some that we may not like at all. The only way another person can even come close to singing our love song, however, is for us to tell that person what we like. Then we must be willing to let the other person decide which of our favorite tunes they want to sing for us.

Chances are good that our mate is singing love songs that we haven't yet learned to hear or appreciate. Perhaps our mate sings a quiet song of reliability, of loyalty, of quiet devotion, of personal sacrifice. Have you tried to identify your mate's love songs?

5. Revealing values and preferences. Revealing our values to each other tells a lot about us. Prioritizing what is important to us and then together comparing our priorities helps us become more intimate. Couples are often surprised to discover how little they know about each other's values.

Here is an exercise you can try. Prioritize the following list and have your spouse do the same, independently, adding whatever else is important to each of you that may not be included here. You may want to copy each value onto a separate card for easy sorting. As you compare your respective lists of prioritized values, take time to discuss why you value the things you do. Do not be critical of each other or defensive about your selections. Simply listen with interest to each other in order to better understand your mate.

LIST OF VALUES AND PREFERENCES

Location of residence	Free time
Flexible work schedule	Variety and change
Social activities	Financial security
Intellectual stimulation	Status
Helping others	Recognition
Creativity	Tranquility
Friendship	Independence
Stability	Solitude
Power and authority	Support
Challenge	Influence
Community involvement	Making decisions
Adventure/excitement	Worship

---

6. Revealing beliefs. Sharing what we believe is a very personal matter. We don't always know what we believe. Sometimes we accept certain "beliefs" just because we have been told to do so. At some point in time, for example, our belief in Christ must move from the Jesus we believed in because we trusted our parents or Sunday school teachers, to a deep inner conviction of our own that Jesus is our Redeemer.

Our personal beliefs are a deep part of our identity and can be revealed between spouses to enhance intimacy. Consider with your spouse what you both believe about the following:

God	Marriage	Children	Abortion
Vocation	Love	Missions	Sex
Education	Church	Government	Commitment
Intimacy	Passion	Needs	News
Travel	Recreation	Retirement	Budgeting

The list could be endless. Even if we don't know what we believe about some things, we could share that and discuss matters to help us reach a conclusion in which we could believe. Of course we cannot become experts in everything, but the point here is that mutual sharing facilitates intimacy because it reveals to our mate something more of who we are.

7. Sharing our philosophy of life. When I was in college, I had a professor who gave us an assignment—to write out a philosophy of our own life. Most people would give you a blank stare if you asked them to share this information with you. People tend not to sit down and put these things into writing or discuss them, but it was one of the best assignments I can ever remember doing. What we believe about our purpose in life is very significant to forming our identity. It reveals a lot about who we are and where we are going with our lives.

Because these matters are often not discussed in any specific detail, it is possible to be married for many years to someone whose beliefs about life run counter to our own. Some of us may be afraid to bring up the subject for fear a conflict may arise. By long-term observation, we can know to some degree our mate's philosophy of life. But if these beliefs can be verbalized, the mutual sharing is a vehicle for achieving closeness.

I know that my wife, Arleen, has a strong belief that her purpose in life is to be available to God to work out his purposes through her as he chooses. Her focus is to live and make decisions from this perspective.

My philosophy of life is similar. I believe that God loves me and wants to extend his love to others through me. As I focus on God's love for me, I am better able to love others. I cannot imagine my life having much significance apart from this. However, viewing life from this belief, I have a framework for living, a perspective that helps my life have meaning no matter what situation may arise.

Not only is this important for my own personal stability, but it is also an important point of contact for Arleen and me. Our knowledge of each other on this level is another way for us to be intimate through mutual self-disclosure of our life purposes as we each see them. Sharing on this level gives our lives together special meaning.

We are not born knowing our purpose in life. Our sense of purpose usually evolves over time and will change as we grow and mature in our thinking. Some of this change will probably occur while we are married, as we share and interact with our mate. Sharing our own discoveries may be helpful and stimulating to our mate, who may seek out his or her own conclusions. Since you have read this book thus far, you are most likely a reflective person and, I hope, married to one. So think about how to share your own sense of purpose with your mate and see how it helps you to sing a revealing love song.

Self-disclosure is the heart of intimacy. By revealing ourselves to our mate, we are singing a love song of intimacy to our beloved. Intimacy is minimized when there are areas that cannot be discussed between a husband and wife. Continuous self-disclosure alone, however, does not make a relationship. Both husband and wife must be open with each other, and that continuous mutual revelation is impossible if our self-disclosures are not well received.

No one will feel safe enough to open up his or her vulnerable heart if previous attempts to do so have been poorly received. Along with mutual self-disclosure, we must also learn how to sing the love song of acceptance. That is the topic of our next chapter.

CHAPTER SEVEN

The Accepting
Love Song

We have discussed how intimacy is important to loving because we can only love a person to the degree that we know him or her. Therefore it is important for us to reveal ourselves to each other on many different levels. However, even if we are successful in disclosing ourselves to one another, we don't always get the response that we would like. In order for us to trust each other with personal thoughts, feelings, and dreams, we need to experience each other's response as understanding, caring, and accepting.

What is *acceptance* in the context of marital intimacy? Acceptance is listening to our mate with sensitivity, interest, and respect. It means to embrace what our mate says to us in such a way that he or she feels safe to continue revealing without fear of judgment, criticism, or ridicule. Acceptance is another way we sing our love song to our mate. Furthermore, it is the one thing above all else that promotes self-disclosure and, therefore, intimacy.

On the other hand, *rejection* in the context of marriage is failing to embrace our mate's expression of thoughts and feelings, treating personal disclosures as useless or insignificant.

Some spouses are "acceptors" and others are "rejecters." Most people are unaware of which category they fall into most of the time. The purpose of this chapter is to help readers become more conscious of their own tendencies toward acceptance or rejection and to enhance marital intimacy by increasing "acceptance" skills. This is the love song of acceptance.

Rejection in marriage can be blatant or subtle. Strange as it may seem, rejection can be obvious to one party and not so obvious to the other. Robin reported that her husband Richard told her she wasn't worth anything. To Richard this was objective truth, and he felt she was being overly sensitive to this comment. She was deeply hurt by the remark and considered him to be insensitive and rejecting. Because our perceptions can differ so radically, we need guidelines to help us assess our own level of sensitivity or insensitivity. Our concern here is with how we can become better "acceptors" and do less rejecting.

SUBTLE REJECTION

In order to better learn how to be accepting of our mate, let us examine some of the typical mistakes people make in dealing with each other.

Imagine that Fred comes home from work in a bad mood and starts complaining to Susan about his job.

Fred: *"I feel terrible. I don't think anybody at work values my opinions."*

The following statements represent different ways that Susan might respond. Would you respond in any of the following ways?

1. "Oh, that reminds me! Our neighbor is upset and wants to speak with you—something about some advice you gave him."
This response ignores Fred's feelings. Susan has related to him in a businesslike manner. When a person shares upset feelings, it is best to deal with the feelings first. It shows loving

kindness and helps the upset person resolve his feelings so that he can think more clearly about the other concerns.

Of course, not only is Susan neglecting to relate to Fred's discouragement, but she's telling him something that will add to his discouragement. Fred must face the neighbor eventually, but she needn't dump this on him when he is already down. If she were to let him talk about his feelings first, he would recover faster from his discouragement and be better prepared to deal with his neighbor.

Let's look at another way Susan might respond. It might help to refer back to Fred's statement before you read each response.

2. *"Oh, I am sure that isn't true, dear."*

This response at least attempts to be supportive. However it still negates Fred's right to his own feelings. Fred has revealed his *feeling* as well as his *belief* upon which his feeling is based. Susan is disagreeing with his belief and ignoring his feeling. It makes him feel even more upset because it is essentially a subtle rejection of what he feels. Because this response looks supportive on the surface, Fred may not even understand why he feels badly about it. Fred needs acceptance that this is how he feels at this moment. He wants empathy and understanding (which Susan may or may not want to give him). However focusing on his belief rather than on what he feels may make Fred uneasy about opening up in the future.

I am not saying that feelings should always be indulged to the exclusion of responsible behavior. However, if we respond sensitively to the feelings first, our spouse will feel cared for and supported and will get over the feeling faster. Unfortunately most of us want to run in and resolve everything immediately without accepting our mate's feelings of the moment.

3. *"That's the way I feel all the time."*

Susan is being a "rejector" here because she had taken the

attention away from Fred and put it on herself. This comment may be true, but the problem is in the timing. If she had wanted Fred to understand this about her, she could have initiated sharing this information on many occasions.

Before we shift the attention to ourselves, it is more supportive to relate first to the feelings that have just been expressed by our mate. When we choose to talk about ourselves in the context of our mate's pain, we are treating them as if their feelings are unimportant to us. This trains them to quit sharing with us, which undermines our intimacy. This subtle rejection discourages our mate from being open with us in the future, since we might "steal the spotlight" again.

4. *"Maybe you don't speak up enough."*

In this response, Susan is trying to fix Fred's problem so he won't feel so bad. Again, this looks very kind on the surface. However, Fred wasn't asking for advice as much as he was sharing his feelings to get some support. Advice is generally not supportive when it isn't desired or requested. When we give advice to people who are not asking for it, we are probably not being sensitive to their feelings.

It can be insulting to give unsolicited advice. This is because it implies that we don't believe the person can figure it out. If we want to give unasked for advice, we might say, "would you like to know what I would do in this situation?" If they show interest in our viewpoint, we haven't insulted them. If they seem disinterested, we need to respect that. Otherwise we are not tuning in to their real needs of the moment. Prolonged treatment of this kind can cause people to withdraw. It can turn revealers into concealers.

5. *"That's not hard to believe."*

The direct put-down is obviously insensitive. Some people do this as a joke and aren't to be taken seriously. But generally this response seeks to avoid intimacy. Susan is putting Fred down so he won't want to discuss it any further. This way she won't have to deal with his feelings, which make her uncomfortable. It is not recommended as a way of encouraging a person who has just revealed feelings of pain and distress.

6. *"Well, it's their loss."*

You are probably wondering what could possibly be wrong with this statement. What is left for a person to say? This statement isn't really too bad. Its weakest feature is that it tries to resolve things too quickly and distracts from attending to the person's feelings in the moment.

This statement is actually supportive and would be appropriate later in the conversation when the discussion is coming to an end.

7. *"I'm sorry you're feeling so bad, dear. What exactly happened at work to make you feel so awful?"*

This is Susan's best response. In this response Susan shows her love for Fred by letting him be the center of attention until he can feel understood and comforted. She is showing interest by asking him to elaborate. Most people would feel safe to reveal more with this response from Susan.

Fred wanted to feel understood and accepted. He didn't need Susan to fix his problem or make him feel different. He just wanted her to comfort him by listening to his feelings. He will work his way through them in his own time.

We often underestimate the power of listening. People need someone to care and just to be with them in times of trouble. Although many of us feel helpless or uncomfortable just listening, it is often the most kind and loving thing we can do.

PARALLEL MONOLOGUES

Many times couples get into mutually rejecting communication patterns and keep it up for years without even realizing what they are doing. Gary and Doris were such a couple. There were a lot of good things about their marriage. They were both extremely autonomous and had a lot to say to each other. But they both enjoyed talking more than listening. They weren't really relating well at all. In subtle ways, they were both rejectors.

Consider the following conversation between Gary and Doris.

Gary: *I ran out of gas on the freeway today. I was so mad at myself and embarrassed when the highway patrolman stopped me to give me a ticket.*

Doris: *Jane and I had lunch together today. I haven't seen her in so long. It just seems like we are getting too busy for our own good. It was wonderful to see her.*

Gary: *I sure am glad to be home.*

Doris: *I have to go to work early tomorrow. I'm really not looking forward to it. It's going to be such a long day.*

In this example, we have two people revealing themselves pretty well. The potential for intimacy is great. The problem here is that neither is relating to what the other has said. In this kind of "parallel monologue," the listener isn't relating to the speaker, leaving doubt about the listener's true involvement in the relationship. Even if every word was heard, the close connection which produces intimacy has been undermined by the absence of any verbal response to what the other has shared.

Not relating directly to what has been said implies disinterest or not caring. Intimacy cannot survive in an indifferent, uncaring environment. Yet people can be married for years without recognizing what is missing in their conversation.

Let's take another look at how this conversation might sound if both Gary and Doris were to relate to each other instead of simply having parallel monologues.

Gary: *I ran out of gas on the freeway today. I was so mad at myself and embarrassed when the highway patrolman stopped me to give me a ticket.*

Doris: *Oh, no! As if one problem wasn't enough! Well, I wouldn't have given you a ticket, even if you deserved it.*

Gary: *Well, that's good to know! Where were you when I needed you?*

Doris: *Jane and I had lunch together today. I haven't seen her in so long. It just seems like we're getting too busy for our own good. It was wonderful to see her.*

Gary: *I'm glad you got to see her. I know what a good friend she has been to you. I'm sure she enjoyed seeing you as well. I sure am glad to be home with you.*

Doris: *I'm glad you are home with me too.... I have to go in to work early tomorrow. I'm really not looking forward to it. It's going to be such a long day....*

Can you tell the difference between these two examples? Most people would be encouraged to continue their self-disclosure in the second context more than in the first. It provides acceptance and involvement while the first tends to isolate and ignore the other partner.

Showing our mate that we heard what was said, and responding to the content before we change the subject is an affirmation of our spouse. This is one way we sing our love song of acceptance to our mate.

EFFECTIVE LISTENING

When we are more eager to be heard than to hear, our communication suffers. We are thinking more about what we want to say than about what is being said. These kinds of discussions are fruitless. The less we feel understood, the harder we hammer away to make our mate hear us. As two voices clamor to keep up with each other, neither feels that the other cares about what the other is saying.

In normal conversations one person speaks, then the other. They go back and forth, assuming that the other listened and understood what was meant. However, in my counseling practice I find that people do not listen to each other as well as they like to think they do. When I ask them to repeat in their own words what they hear their spouse saying, many people have difficulty with this. So I suggest that they try the following exercise, which is simple in concept, but difficult to integrate into everyday conversations:

1. The husband (or wife) says what is on his (her) mind.

2. The wife puts into her own words what she hears her husband saying and responds with statements such as:
   "What I hear you saying is...."
   "Are you telling me that...?"

3. The husband either clarifies a point, or says he feels understood:
   "Well, I don't mean to put so much emphasis on the last part. What I mean to say is...."
   "Yes, it sounds like you understand what I mean."

4. The wife then proceeds with what is on her mind, as in step 1.

5. The husband responds as in step 2:
   "Are you basically saying that...?"

This exercise is not intended for simple conversation such as "please pass the salt." But it is excellent for those moments when the discussion is complex or emotional.

Some criticize this exercise as too contrived and unrealistic for day-to-day living. I will agree that it feels awkward at first. But most things feel awkward initially, especially if we are trying to counter old habits. However, those who learn to work with it are usually grateful. I challenge you to give it your best effort.

It may take a third party or a counselor to keep you on track initially. As simple as this procedure may sound, couples tend to get caught up so strongly in making a point that staying with the exercise becomes difficult, especially when emotions are aroused.

Making the effort to really hear and understand our mate is another way that we can sing a love song of acceptance.

ACCEPTANCE IS NOT AGREEMENT

Being good acceptors for our mate not only involves receiving our partner's feelings, but also that person's thoughts and ideas. This does not mean that we necessarily agree, but that we accept other's right to view things in a personal way without our judgment or criticism.

We perceive situations differently. Just because our mate thinks that it is time for a new car doesn't mean we have to agree. However, acceptance means we are willing to listen to his or her thoughts on the matter without getting defensive or putting down the idea. I have watched many married people sabotage their own purposes simply by not respecting what their mates had to say without instantly beating it down.

Many times we are willing to give up our own ideas once we have been able to talk about them openly in an accepting environment. Actually, once we hear ourselves talk about it, we may come to our own conclusion that it is not a good idea at this time. Instant disagreement virtually invites opposition. People resent not being accepted.

If however, our mate still clings to the idea of getting a new car, we can express our thoughts on the matter in a loving way without putting our mate down for having their own feelings and desires. We might say, "I would love to see you have a car like that, honey. Nothing would make me happier. But it makes me nervous to think about taking on more payments right now, especially with our taxes coming due next month. What do you think?"

We may think it's a good idea or we may think it's a bad one. Sometimes we need to rethink our own position. We each have to decide for ourselves. The point is that one way we sing our love song to our mate is to accept his or her opinions as valid.

Two people from two different backgrounds are not going to think alike about everything. Even if we married the schoolmate next door, there will be family differences. This is one of the things that makes marriage so interesting. A difference in values or beliefs doesn't have to create a problem as long as we respect each other's right to personal opinions.

Sometimes we may be afraid to be different from our mate. We fear that if we don't think alike, we won't be accepted. This may be based on actual experience. But if we need our spouse to approve of us that much, then we will not be able to enjoy each other's uniqueness. This is why the autonomous love song is a necessary counterpoint to the accepting love song.

ACCEPTANCE AND BEHAVIOR

We have discussed accepting our mate's thoughts and feelings. What about behavior?

In marital loving, we must accept our spouse without trying to change him or her. Maybe you get irritated when your mate doesn't replace the toilet paper or gets bread crumbs in the butter dish. We can tell our mate how that behavior affects us, but we must accept whatever response we receive. We can't expect to change all of our mate's ungracious habits.

Some of us make the mistake of telling our mate what he or she should do to make us happy. However this tends to build walls since it is not accepting of the other. Attempts to control each other create distance, not intimacy. We can share how we are affected by our mate's behavior, but it is better to leave their response up to him or her.

Sharon felt badly because she perceived Ron as uncaring about her feelings. She would give him a list of possible gifts she would enjoy for her birthday, but he would purchase something not on her list that he might enjoy having himself, such as a portable television, calculator, or candy.

Ron's selfishness is not the issue at the moment. My point

here is the way Sharon tries to resolve her problem. Her method is to demand that Ron only buy her gifts from her list:

> "Ron, I gave you a list of gifts to choose from. Why can't you pick something from the list that you know I will like? I just don't think you care!"

Sharon is making the mistake of trying to control Ron's behavior by telling him exactly what to do so that she will feel better. Furthermore, her tone and attitude only make Ron defensive and angry.

It is easy to understand why Sharon would do this. She is hurting. She wants to feel loved. However, she is dictating her terms to Ron, instead of letting him sing his love song in his own way. To tell Ron how to sing his love song to her is to control him, which will push him away and undermine any efforts toward intimacy.

If Sharon wants to sing a love song of her own, she will reveal her hurts and disappointments to Ron without demanding that he sing his love song her way. Control kills love, while vulnerable self-disclosure gives love more freedom to function on its own.

Sharon would probably do much better if she simply shared with Ron what she would like in the future without blaming him for the past:

> "Ron, I feel really close to you when you buy me a gift that you know I will enjoy. I hope you will find my list of gift ideas helpful."

If he continues to disregard her list, she may have to share how his behavior is affecting her:

> "Ron, it really hurts me when you buy presents that you will enjoy more than I will. I need you to be more sensitive to my feelings and interests when you are buying me a gift."

In this way, Sharon is both revealing her feelings and accepting Ron's right to determine his own behavior. People often get confused at this point. It seems to some that sharing feelings is the same as telling another how to behave. But there is a difference between revealing and demanding. Revealing is a way of making our desires known. It is an intimate act to let our mate know how we feel. There is no guarantee that we will get what we want when we reveal. Revealing is vulnerable self-disclosure without controlling our mate's response. On the other hand, a demand is telling our mate specifically how to be and what to do to meet our need.

Acceptance of our mate's behavior, assuming it is non-violent or not destructive, is a way of loving him or her. This acceptance of thoughts, feelings, and behavior promotes acceptance and intimacy in relationships.

Are you a revealer or a demander, an acceptor or a rejector?

We know that marital intimacy is detailed personal familiarity with our mate. We have seen how the love song of intimacy is the completion and fulfillment of the love song of passion. Intimacy can be achieved through the love songs of mutual self-disclosure and mutual acceptance. Intimacy is being safely known.

The following is a poem I wrote to my wife on our anniversary one year:

SAFELY KNOWN

I can speak with confidence
about my love for you,
for you love me and accept me,
though you know me through and through.

You see me when I'm up and down,
you know me inside out;
the way I think, the way I feel,
you know what I'm about.

Yet you accept me anyway,
you love me as your own.
this is why I love you dear—
I feel so safely known.

I share with you my heart of hearts,
because you'll understand.
When I think I'll fall apart,
you'll lend a helping hand.

When I need a little lift,
and call you on the phone,
once again I'll find your gift,
that I am safely known.

When I doubt myself at times,
when I fear I'll fail,
your belief in me, my love,
Puts wind back in my sail.

You bring out the best in me,
Your seeds of faith are sown;
Because you have believed in me,
I feel so safely known.

Safely known, intimate, fueled by passion... There is yet another love song that needs to be sung for a Christian marriage to go the distance. Marital love needs the protection found in the love song of commitment. That is the subject of the final section of this book.

SECTION III

The Love Song of Commitment

CHAPTER EIGHT

The Biblical
Love Song

Keith looked handsome as he stood at waiting for his bride at the front of the church. His eyes twinkled and his smile grew broad when he saw his lovely wife-to-be appear at the back of the church. Keith and Mary had been looking forward to this moment with great expectation. Having already shared their dreams, their values, their hopes and fears, they were now confirming before witnesses their commitment to journey through life together.

As their desire to be together grew, they were both certain that heaven had arranged for them to meet. They didn't know what lay ahead. After the wedding, they continued to reveal their hearts to one another and to accept each other with loving tenderness, affirming their commitment to each other regularly.

Keith became a busy pastor in a local church, and they began a family. Neither Keith nor Mary could ever have imagined what was to follow. Four years and two children later, Mary suffered a debilitating attack of polio which left her a quadriplegic.

In spite of this catastrophe, they both maintained their belief that God had a purpose in bringing them together. Their relationship remained a priority and they found meaning in working together for constructive solutions to their personal problems. They believe to this day that as Christians they are to be a picture of Christ to the world. They see their relationship as a lifelong commitment to God and to each other.

Keith and Mary believe that the best basis for commitment in marriage is what we can *give* to the relationship, rather than what we can *get* from it. Of course, giving and getting are two halves of the same equation. However, when our wants take precedence over giving, our marital commitment will not be at its maximum strength.

This biblical love song does not stop giving when it stops getting. If our love were merely an echo in response to the love we receive from others, love could die out in a hurry. Love can be inspired by others, but loving with *agape* love is not conditional upon getting love back.

LOVE IN THE BIBLE

The Bible has a lot to say about love. In 1 John 3:18 we read, "Dear children, let us not love with words or tongue but with actions...."

What kind of actions demonstrate love? What does love look like, according to the Scriptures? It is appropriate that we look closely at what the Bible tells us about love.

The most often-quoted biblical reference on love is the apostle Paul's beautiful love chapter in his first letter to the Corinthians. It is helpful to understand the context in which he wrote. Paul is responding to reports he had heard about factions forming in the Corinthian church. He frames his remarks on love with that specific situation in mind.

Without pretending to achieve the impossible—an exhaustive description of love—he mentions some of their behaviors that are *not* characteristic of love as well as some behaviors that *are*. Let us look at those mentioned in chapter thirteen of Paul's first letter to the Corinthian church.

1. Love is patient (1 Cor 13:4, 7). According to Dr. Kenneth Bailey,[1] when Paul speaks of patience, he uses two different Greek words for our English word. The first use of "patience," found in verse four, has to do with *self-control.*

Paul is saying that when we have the power to strike out destructively in anger but do not do it, we act lovingly by controlling ourselves. Personal restraint in a moment of anger is an act of loving patience. For example, a husband is acting in love when he refrains from yelling at his wife who has just damaged their new car.

Can you remember the last time you felt like saying something out of anger but did not? This kind of self-control does not mean that we never share our feelings. Rather, it means we have control of *how* we share our feelings.

The other meaning of loving patience is used by Paul in verse seven. This has to do with feeling vulnerable and not being in control of what is happening to us. Paul is saying that love perseveres even when under stress.

When Mary became ill, Keith felt stressed and Mary felt vulnerable. This was a perfect recipe for trouble. Keith wrote about it in his book *Not a Sometimes Love.*[2] Although it was a struggle for them, both were committed to talking and working things out. They were both patient with themselves and with each other in facing their difficult and discouraging situation.

Love perseveres even when it is uncomfortable to be doing so. We sing our love song by managing our own pain because we love our mate more than we require the comfort of immediate resolution.

So love is patient in two ways: through self-control and through a tolerant attitude when we are not in control of our circumstances.

2. Love is kind (1 Cor 13:4, Gal 5:22). Kindness means being courteous, considerate, and gentle. Love is not abusive or insensitive to the needs and feelings of others. Love demonstrates respect and caring for our mate. When asking our mate for something without blaming him or her for being negligent in the past, we are being kind. When we awaken our spouse gently in the morning rather than abruptly, we are showing kindness. Opening the car door for our wife, or asking our husband how things went for him at work is being kind. Allowing him to not discuss the subject if he chooses not to being kind. Keeping ourselves looking clean and appealing for our spouse is another form of kindness.

Kindness is only one of the many love songs we can sing to our mate. What form of lovingkindness can you show to your husband or wife right now?

3. Love is supportive (1 Cor 13:4). I have changed Paul's wording ("love is not jealous or envious") in order to continue looking at love in terms of what we can *do*, how love motivates and empowers us to behave. Since biblical love is action, Paul only uses "feeling" words to describe what love is *not*. Taking the liberty of stating his meaning in positive terms, we can realize that our love song should be supportive of our mate.

Jealousy and envy are rooted in fear about who we are. God has not given us the spirit of fear, but of love, power, and a sound mind (see 2 Timothy 1:7). Furthermore perfect love casts out fear (see 1 John 4:18).

Love, then, is not jealous or envious because it is not fearful. As loving persons, we are confident in who we are as children of God and children of love. We believe in our own significance as married lovers committed to each other's well-being.

Hence we are supportive of our mate's talents, gifts, and good fortune even if it means that they enjoy more "success" than we do. I remember seeing more than one movie on this theme: a man divorces a woman he loves because he can't stand the shame he feels over being less successful than his famous wife.

It is significant for us to be successful in our role as supporter, rejoicing with him or her. Public recognition should not be our criteria for success. Knowing we are fulfilling our created purpose as conduits of God's love is our ultimate success.

Mary knows that her wheelchair does not rob her of her power to love Keith. She is not jealous or envious of Keith because she knows her significance is not limited to her physical mobility. She has grown to recognize that her life as a wife to Keith is meaningful as a confidante, encourager, and prayer partner. She can still be passionate about her desire to be intimate with him. They enjoy intimate moments of verbal and physical contact. They are benevolent toward one another.

4. Love is humble (1 Cor 13:4). Humility is a key word in the New Testament because it represents the opposite of pride, the very essence of sin. Pride is accepting for oneself honor and status that belong only to God.[3]

Pride is not a love song. It is a superficial effort to feel good about oneself by appearing to be better than others. Pride is usually due to overcompensating for one's deep inner self-doubt. Pride is wrong because it lacks faith in God that we are significant, and it seeks approval from the very people it demeans. Humility is recognizing that we are nothing apart from what God has given to us. Thus we approach other people with a perspective of equality and responsibility for mutual acceptance.

Christian humility is a lack of concern for one's own prestige.[4] People who are well-grounded, who know who they are and believe in their value as a loving child of God, do not need to resort to boasting, which only draws attention to their self-doubt. The sad thing about our society is that there are many great people in life about whom we never get to hear because they are too humble to toot their own horns. The ones we are forced to hear about are the approval-seekers who get attention because they actively seek it.

In marriage, pride makes a husband or wife afraid to ask for what he or she wants. A humble spouse can make requests without making demands. Then the person accepts whatever is given and seeks to give whatever possible to meet the needs of the partner. Some people think that having to ask is the same as begging or groveling. But begging is pleading to get what you want. Asking is not begging because once we ask, we accept whatever response we get without insisting on getting our own way.

Pride is a superficial attempt to feel significant. Pride is afraid to look bad. James found it difficult to apologize when he spoke hurtfully toward his wife. This of course hurt her even more. James loved his pride more than his bride.

5. Love is courteous and respectful (1 Cor 13:5). Opening a door for one's wife may seem old-fashioned to some, but it is a symbolic act of respect for the wife. Not interrupting conversations is an act of courtesy. Helping our mate carry in groceries from the garage is another courtesy.

Love is courteous because it respects the other person and cares about the other's feelings as well as their physical well-being. Love is respectful; we can treat each other with dignity, acknowledging everyone's worth in the eyes of God.

6. Love is generous, gracious, and unselfish (1 Cor 13:5). "Love does not seek its own," writes Paul. This does not mean that we cannot be concerned about our own needs. Taking charge of meeting our own needs is being responsible. We are taught here not to put our own needs ahead of another person. Instead we are to be sensitive to the needs of our mate and respond graciously and generously to him or her.

When it is time to go out with our mate, are we willing to participate in an activity of his or her choice? Who usually gets to choose what to do? Is it balanced? Are we both willing to share these opportunities? When our needs conflict, how do we decide what to do? Are we generous and giving?

Emotional maturity requires that we honestly face our needs

and desires, yet also be willing to forego their satisfaction from time to time in order to care about our mate's needs.

When was the last time you set your need aside in deference to your mate?

7. Love is honest and just, rejoicing with truth (1 Cor 13:6). Honesty is important in marriage because it builds trust. Deceit breaks down trust and communication. To walk rightly and speak what is right (see Isaiah 33:15) is the loving path, although it isn't always easy.

Two people cannot be each other's primary support system if they are not going to be honest with each other. Love cares about the other and provides stability by sharing the truth. Even when the truth hurts, at least our mate will know what he or she is dealing with. Deceit makes it impossible for anyone to deal with reality because it is concealed.

Love is willing to face whatever feelings are necessary in order to be honest. When Keith and Mary shared their mutual frustrations with each other it was painful. Keith needed Mary to let him sleep. Yet Mary needed Keith to help her in the middle of the night. By sharing their mutual frustrations, they could face them together, hurt together, and love together.

Whether we fear our mate's reactions, are embarrassed about something we did, or feel guilty or ashamed, honesty allows love to respond in a way that deceit does not. Lies prevent intimacy from developing. This, in turn, slams the door shut on love. Honesty, however, is disclosure, which is where love and intimacy begin.

8. Love is trusting (1 Cor 13:7). Love is not only reliable and trustworthy. Love honors the beloved with trust as well. Trust builds unity and oneness. It is when trust has been violated that it is most difficult to restore. Most of us think that we cannot trust someone who has proven untrustworthy on some occasion. But trust is a lot like loving. We may not *feel* loving or trusting but we can still *act* loving and trusting.

If a situation feels trustworthy or safe, it doesn't require much trust on our part. Trust is almost meaningless without some risk. I can say that I trust the chair I am sitting on, but that doesn't require much trust since that is the purpose of a chair. To trust our mate to not hurt us again after embarrassing us is another matter. This takes a lot more trust than sitting in a chair. It is a bold choice to trust.

A relationship cannot deepen in intimacy without trust. We must trust our mate to accept us if we are to risk self-disclosure and fulfill our desire for closeness.

9. Love is forgiving (1 Cor 13:5). Love "keeps no record of wrongs." It does not hold a grudge or seek to get even. Love forgives because God is love and God has forgiven us. We are compelled to forgive our spouse and to release him or her from any liability for the harm we have suffered.

Have you forgiven your mate for his or her insensitivity toward you recently? For the hurtful comment made toward you? Are you dwelling on the thought that you didn't deserve it? Or are you aware of the opportunity to love your mate by forgiving?

"Do you have to cook this meal so often?" you are asked when you worked all day and didn't feel like cooking at all. Your first impulse is to throw the meal on the floor and walk out of the room. However you decide to manage your own hurt. "Of course not, dear. But it is an easy meal to prepare after a long day's work. Why don't you help me next time and we can fix something that we both like better?"

10. Love protects (1 Cor 13:7). The phrase (KJV) "Beareth all things" is rendered in the NIV as love "always protects." Dr. Kenneth Bailey points out that love doesn't "leak."[5] It keeps out what should be kept out and keeps in what should be kept in. For example, when we are truly loving, we will not allow another person to come between us and our mate. Our love will protect our relationship from another relationship. We will remain faithful to each other. We will keep out what doesn't belong between us.

Dr. Bailey also points out that love does not allow to leak out what should be kept inside the relationship. If our mate tells us a secret in confidence, our love will not leak out that secret to another. Love protects from leaking out.

It should be pointed out, however, that love is not overprotective. Love does not shield others from accepting responsibility for their own behavior. Love does not do for us what we should be learning to do for ourselves. Love holds us accountable for our actions.

11. Love hopes (1 Cor 13:7). Hope is the fuel of passion. Without hope, passion dwindles to nothing. The desire to be close to our mate needs the hope of at least occasional fulfillment. Love hopes for opportunities to be expressed. Love hopes for the best for the beloved. Love hopes to serve in all the ways mentioned above.

MORE BIBLICAL LOVE NOTES

Now that we have surveyed 1 Corinthians 13, let us look at other New Testament exhortations to love.

1. Love builds up (1 Thes 5:11). Paul wants us to "encourage one another and build each other up...." Furthermore, in 1 Corinthians 14:3 Paul connects encouragement and comfort with strengthening as if to say that one implies the other. So loving our spouse means to help build up and strengthen our mate with comfort and encouragement.

When our mate can't seem to find work, do we dump our anxieties and criticize him or her for not finding a job? Or do we offer affection and reassurance with words of trust, confidence, and belief in the one we love? Enjoying our mate's presence even when he or she is discouraged requires autonomy on our part. This can have a powerful regenerative effect on our partner, which gives him or her renewed strength and courage to keep trying.

Sometimes just being a good listener is the best way to console. If we are truly available to listen, our mate may begin to see things differently as he or she puts thoughts into complete sentences.

The Bible reveals many ways to encourage, comfort, and build up our mate:

Rejoice with those who rejoice; mourn with those who mourn (Rom 12:15).

Bear with the failings of the weak and not to please ourselves (Rom 15:1).

Warn those who are idle, encourage the timid, help the weak, be patient with everyone. Make sure that nobody pays back wrong for wrong, but always try to be kind to each other (1 Thes 5:14-15).

Carry each other's burdens (Gal 6:2).

This is what Paul means about building each other up.

2. Love serves. In John 13:14, Jesus says, "Now that I, your Lord and Teacher, have washed your feet, you also should wash one another's feet." It is not customary or meaningful in our culture to go around washing other people's feet. The point is to be thoughtful and responsive in serving others, even in menial ways. Offering a cup of coffee or a glass of water to someone is a small example of serving. Giving somebody a ride when they lack transportation, or just listening to somebody share his sadness when you would rather be somewhere else are also examples.

Galatians 5:13 tells us to serve one another in love. Pete helps Sylvia with the housework and Sylvia works to supplement the family income. They serve each other.

1 John 3:17 tells us to give our material possessions to our brother in need. People in our church bring canned and dried foods every Sunday which are taken to a local food bank to serve the hungry. Churches in our area take turns housing homeless people who are trying to save enough money to get back on their feet.

These are examples of loving through service.

3. Love is faithful (Gal 5:22). Love does not say one thing and do another. It is reliable and steadfast. Love is loyal and trustworthy. Love believes in itself and will not violate its own integrity or the trust that others place in it. Love follows through with its promises. It is consistent in its caring for another's welfare.

Whether we promise to pick up the children from school, go to the market on the way home from work, or remember our mate's birthday, we are loving when we are faithful. We provide stability for each other when we are so reliable that our mate knows what he or she can expect.

Keith has been faithful to Mary for over forty years. He stayed with her during her frightening transition from health to disability. He has also been faithful from day to day to see that she is cared for while he is at work.

Mary has been faithful also. Emotionally, it has not been easy for her to accept her plight. She has trusted God to give her meaning and purpose for her life under these terribly restricting circumstances. Furthermore, she has been faithful in praying for and supporting Keith emotionally in his demanding job as a minister. But more than that, God has opened opportunities for ministry for her as well, in teaching on marriage, developing a women's ministry, and assisting Keith in premarital and marriage seminars. Because of Mary's attitude and God's love, she continued to grow even through her disability.

There are other ways that love is faithful. If we meet somebody we find to be more interesting than our mate, loving commitment for our mate motivates faithfulness. We may need professional help in dealing with our feelings, but love behaves in a faithful manner.

4. Marital love is sexual (1 Cor 7:3-5). When the apostle Paul admonished the husbands and wives in the Corinthian church not to deprive each other of sexual relations, he did not mean to imply that there would never be situations where abstinence would be appropriate. Paul was speaking in the context of a sexually permissive society where prostitutes were used in worship to pagan deities. Paul was speaking about not associating with sexually immoral people (5:9).

In seeking to be clear about basic instruction for an immature and confused church, Paul was telling the average couple to limit their sexual expression of love to each other. He was advocating regular sexual relations in the context of marriage. Obviously regular sexual relations with our spouse makes it easier to remain faithful when society around us is encouraging immorality.

Couples who abstain from sexual relations out of respect for each other's needs are showing love to one another. However, a husband or wife who withholds sexual pleasure out of emotional immaturity and hurt feelings is not acting out of love. Those of us with unresolved problems of this nature should seek counseling from a trusted professional.

Women often ask if they should have intercourse with their husbands when they do not feel close to them. My response depends upon their answers to several questions. Why doesn't she feel close to her husband? Is he abusive? Unpredictably violent? Uncaring? Does he act nice only when he wants her in bed? This is not a loving situation and I do not believe a woman should have to have sexual relations under these conditions.

This couple should seek professional help, although the husband who acts like this will probably not be supportive of going to counseling. I would recommend that the wife initiate counseling on her own. Many times the husband eventually follows. Even though his attitude is not the best initially, many men are surprised at what they learn about themselves. They start to change.

Another consideration as to why a woman may not feel close to her husband is that she might be oversensitive and get her feelings hurt easily. If she tends to hold a grudge or finds it difficult to forgive, even when the husband is normally loving and nonabusive, she should seek help to learn about forgiveness and managing emotional pain. These feelings should not be allowed to interfere with a couple's sexual relationship.

There may be psychological problems that interfere with a woman wanting sex with her husband. Ronda has been unable to make love with her husband ever since she was raped several years ago. She should have sought help much sooner than she did but she was frightened, embarrassed, and uncertain anything could be done. Fortunately she did find healing, but she and her husband were celibate for quite a long time. It would not have been appropriate for her to engage in forced sex relations prior to working through her unresolved pain and fears from this abusive situation.

Recently men have been forming support groups for husbands of sexually abused women. The husbands are victims as well, since their sexual needs are not being satisfied. They need to be able to talk about their concerns with men who can understand their situation.

Finally, there are physiological problems that can make sex undesirable for a partner. When this is the case, sexual relations should not be required, but medical advice should be sought. When sexual problems are of physical origin rather than psychological, it is still possible to have a feeling of closeness between the husband and wife. This is assuming that there is an open line of communication between them. Under these conditions, they sing their love songs to one another without demanding more than the other can give of a sexual nature.

MARITAL COMMITMENT AND GIVING LOVE

Even with this brief survey of the biblical view of love, it is clear that love is a matter of being consistent in our giving to others. Marital commitment is a promise to treat our mate with loving behavior even when it feels difficult to do so. If we believe that marital love is more about giving than getting, then any difficulties our spouse has in loving us should not affect the strength of our marriage. Furthermore, if both husband and wife are committed to *giving* as the criteria for their personal fulfillment in marriage, their marriage will be very sturdy.

When our commitment to someone is based upon how well they perform for us or meet our needs, it makes for a shaky, not a stable relationship. All of us are human; we let each other down at times. However, if we accept the responsibility for our own giving as having deep personal meaning, then both parties enjoy added stability in the relationship.

The Scriptures tell us to love God and others. It is my belief that ultimate fulfillment in life comes from believing in our own significance as representatives of God's love. We have access to the power of God in our lives to love others; as children of God, our lives possess true significance.

If we reflect only upon the immediate pleasure of feeling comfortable and secure, we will become materialistic and superficial in our understanding of life. However, if we look beyond these temporal gratifications to the spiritual dimension for meaning and significance to our lives, we can discover a new kind of fulfillment that makes comfort and security become secondary concerns. This makes the composition of our love songs a truly inspired work of art.

Keith and Mary recognize that their significance and personal fulfillment lie in being committed to God as well as to each other. Marriage for them cannot be separated from a relationship with God. The joy of participating in God's loving purposes is the motivation that inspires their love for each other. Mary's disabled body is a daily reminder to them both of how limited and easily lost are the comforts of this world and life itself. Their fulfillment is at a higher level. Knowing God enables them to find ultimate meaning in their mutual love.

The marriages that have stability and peace amidst pain and struggle are those wherein people believe in the power and significance of their own love. A key word here is "believe," for what we believe makes all the difference in the nature of our commitment. If we believe simply that our needs and personal comfort are the most important basis of our relationship, our marital commitment will rest shakily on this premise. And when our needs and comfort no longer exist, there will be nothing to sustain the relationship. However, if we believe that love and marriage have profound significance for giving meaning to our lives, then our marital commitment will be founded upon something substantial that will carry us through the darkest periods of our lives together as husband and wife.

Keith and Mary understand that tragedy and suffering cannot undermine *agape* love. They realize as they look into the heavens that love is a lot like the stars:

"Sadness is love's very special season,
To share itself more nobly than before;
Like the stars, the darkness is the reason,
Love can shine so brightly all the more."

Eugene Whitney

Exercising our power to love and care for another person can bring us a deep satisfaction. Even if loving another costs us personal sacrifice, and even if the one whom we are loving doesn't recognize it as such and rejects us, we can still find the satisfaction of significance in caring for another.

When Doris made her adulterous husband Dale move out of the house until he was willing to give up his girlfriend, she was misunderstood by Dale as being unloving. This was not the case, however. The most difficult thing for her to do was to ask him to leave because she knew that she might lose him altogether if she forced the issue. But by forcing him to make a decision, she was loving him into being responsible rather than riding the fence. She was loving him by not sponsoring his adulterous behavior. Yet he felt unloved because she was making him uncomfortable. Love, however, is not always comforting or indulgent. As we have already discovered, we must not make decisions based upon what will make people like us. Love acts according to what it believes, not according to what feels good.

Think what the world would be like today if everyone practiced "tough love."[6] It is sad that people do not believe in their own love enough to be firm with their loved ones. Perhaps they never had their love affirmed by anyone.

God himself has loved us with a perfect love of personal sacrifice, gracious forgiveness, and loving acceptance. We human beings, recipients of God's loving attention, are called to imitate God's love. We find our worth in what we believe about God's love toward us. Although we may not always "feel" loving, we can keep ourselves on the loving track by thinking carefully, choosing biblical beliefs about love, and acting upon them. All of our love songs in marriage are based upon our belief in God's love for us.

In this chapter we have reviewed what love looks like according to the New Testament. Marital commitment is a promise to be loving toward our mate. The commitment to love our mate is strongest when it is based upon a belief in the value of our own love song, rather than upon what we can get from our marriage.

Sounds good, doesn't it? Let's build on this principle as we move on to discuss the staying power necessary to strengthen and support such commitment.

CHAPTER NINE

The Enduring
Love Song

As important as it is to sing our love song to our mate, it is not always easy to do. Some people seem easier to love than others. Yet if we are to be committed to our marriage, we must accept responsibility for loving our mate, even when we do not feel like doing so. This is the love song of commitment—living out our love in both good and bad times.

Sometimes there are situations where we would like to believe we are exempt from following through on this promise. Although most people get married expecting the best, an incredible number of couples have second thoughts about their marriage after a few years. Something unexpected often appears in the relationship to make people think they were somehow tricked into a painful partnership that they never wanted. Marriage usually seems like a pretty good idea on the wedding day. Yet, for whatever reasons people marry, most are surprised to discover how things can change over time. When relationships don't work out the way we imagined they would, singing our love song becomes difficult at best.

Jan didn't realize how negative Tom could be until after she married him. Joe hadn't noticed how much Cindy depended on him for things she should be doing for herself. It is amazing how much we are able to overlook when we are under the spell of romantic expectations. Time and experience, however, tend to reveal things as they really are. As we get to know our mate better in the married state, we may realize that we got more than we expected. Sometimes that is good. Sometimes it is not.

The frustration and disappointment people often face present yet another opportunity to sing a love song. Those truly committed to giving are aware that marriage is not so much *finding* the right person as *being* the right person. This is not a simple matter. How can we be the right, loving person God intends for us to be when our marriage, for one reason or another, is a source of pain and disappointment for us?

Although our response is to be one of love, there are different kinds of loving behavior for different situations. All difficult situations should not necessarily be treated alike. For example, the abusive mate should not be treated the same as the mate who is severely ill physically. Yet both present a challenge of disappointment and pain, and both need a loving response. Let us look at a few of these difficult situations and how we might sing our love song even in our pain and disappointment.

THE OVERCOMMITTED SPOUSE

It is wonderful when two people are both committed to their marriage. However, quite often one spouse will also overcommit to activities outside of the marriage. I did it myself just this week. My wife has gently reminded me and I know she is right. Arleen and I both enjoy life and tend to want to do more than we are able. When either of us becomes overinvolved, we both lose.

When Carl and Marilyn came to me for counseling, Marilyn was concerned that Carl was putting in so much time coaching his Little League baseball team. Carl loved baseball and this was a great diversion for him from his daily routine at the office.

However, it took so much time that Marilyn was really feeling unimportant to him.

Carl would say, "I know you want more of my time, Marilyn. But frankly I get a lot out of coaching the boys and I don't want to give it up." Carl enjoyed coaching his baseball team more than he enjoyed his marriage.

Marilyn is a perky, upbeat brunette whom most men would find attractive. She is sensitive and responsive. She was open to self-examination, deeply spiritual, and committed to loving her husband. How does she cope with her overcommitted husband when she is low on his priority list?

We must always keep in mind that no matter what we do, there is no guarantee that we will get what we want. However if we do not try something, we are assuring our own disappointment. Therefore the first step is always to ask for what we want.

Marilyn can say, "Carl, I am glad you enjoy coaching the boys. I can see how important that is for you and I want you to be happy. I try to be independent during these times so that you can enjoy yourself. I even come to some of the games to support you in what you are doing. But I feel a strong need to have your attention sometimes. I need to feel your interest in my life as well. When do you think the two of us could do something together?"

Marilyn may or may not get what she wants, but she has a better chance of having time with her husband if she asks for what she wants in a kind way rather than blaming him for how things have been in the past.

THE ALOOF SPOUSE

An aloof person is distant, withdrawn, and unrevealing. The classical example is the "introvert," who very frequently marries an extrovert. Introverts are not always antisocial. They just like a lot of time alone to think, without having to react to external stimulation. The introvert-extrovert marriage does not have to be a problem unless the individuals are extremely polarized and stubborn.

When Jan and Jerry came to see me for counseling, it was clear that Jerry didn't want to be there. He initiated nothing, never smiled, and answered my questions as briefly and as non-committally as possible.

Jan was an outgoing person who needed attention from other people. She had always thought that Jerry was a good listener. However, over time she became disappointed to realize that Jerry wasn't always listening. In fact, the more she talked, the more he tuned out. Even when he was listening he didn't interact much with what she said.

Jerry was an introvert. Unfortunately, that's partly why he wasn't inclined to speak up about his need to have time alone. His quiet withdrawal made Jan anxious and angry. The more demanding she got, the more stubborn Jerry became in his withdrawal. They became more and more polarized over time, each feeling controlled by the other.

If Jan had paid more attention to Jerry's needs, and if Jerry could have talked more openly about his need for time alone, they could have been more loving to each other.

How can we sing our love song to an aloof spouse? As with any person we love, we must be sensitive to that person's needs as well as to our own. We need to tell him or her that we recognize the need for privacy and time alone, but that we have a need for intimate conversation and sharing of feelings. The aloof spouse may not be able to give us what we want, but it is still our responsibility to reveal what we want, providing the chance to respond.

It is important to remember that blaming our aloof mate will only make him or her withdraw even more. We may have to ask questions and wait patiently for our mate to think before they respond. Those of us who are very verbal often lose patience with a quiet mate. We may not be comfortable with silence, but we must learn to be patient and recognize that everyone is not able to express themselves as quickly as we might like.

Actually Jerry wanted to be more expressive. He lived in constant emotional pain and embarrassment over his inability to speak more confidently. In Jerry's case, he had been rejected by his parents and raised by his grandparents, who totally dominated him. They always had to be the center of attention, so early on Jerry had learned that there was never any room for his feelings to be expressed in their presence. Jerry never learned to expect anyone to care about what he had to say. Thus he failed to develop a natural fluency in revealing himself.

Jan didn't understand the extent of Jerry's difficulty when she married him. She took his aloofness personally. Jan had to learn that to sing her love song to Jerry she was going to have to accept his needs for time to himself and seek more social involvement with her girlfriends. This would meet some of her needs that Jerry is not able to satisfy. As she becomes more sensitive to Jerry and less demanding, she has a better chance of him opening up to her.

THE CONTROLLING SPOUSE

Some people find themselves with a marital partner who likes to control everything. Such was the case for Doreen. She always thought Dennis was such a gentleman and admired him for always knowing what to do in every situation. However, once they were married, she began to feel like a 10-watt light bulb next to a 100-watt light bulb. She felt that he outshined her entirely, as if her presence made no difference to him at all. When they were out in public together she felt secure with his leadership. However, in the privacy of their home she perceived these same traits as domineering and controlling. Doreen couldn't cope with his dominance.

While Dennis was very much as Doreen described him, she

was part of her own problem by never letting Dennis know how she felt. Actually, he would back down when she would speak up about how he was affecting her. He would even respond appropriately when he was aware of what she wanted. What he did not do was to attempt to read her mind. He assumed she would speak out on her own behalf as he did for himself. However, Doreen found it difficult to ask for what she wanted. Able to keep her feelings "bottled up" for a limited time, Doreen would eventually explode. She would act as if she really had no expectation of being heard on a normal level. As she burst forth in a sudden tirade of yelling and screaming, Dennis, with his mouth hanging open in astonishment, would wonder what in the world had set her off.

Both of them needed to take more responsibility for their own behavior. Doreen needed to stand up to her controlling spouse. For example, instead of fuming because she had to prepare the evening meal alone after working all day, Doreen could say, "Dennis, I am working on the meat and potatoes. Would you please make us a salad?"

Many of us who feel dominated have felt this way throughout our lives. Because we don't feel we have any control, we automatically react defensively in the face of the authority of others. However, if we remain calm, firm, and pleasant, we might be surprised at the response we get.

It is always easier to blame another for being controlling, but blame often reflects our fear of not being taken seriously. Those of us who fail to accept our own authority to speak up on our own behalf should not be surprised when the force of a dominant personality overwhelms us. Letting our mate know how we are affected by his or her actions and attitudes can help counter our defenseless feelings in the face of our mate's power. Only when we develop a sense of our own autonomy and exercise our own authority does the fear of speaking up subside.

THE CRITICAL SPOUSE

Some people complain of having a spouse who is critical. Before we are too quick to diagnose our mate as critical, however, we must evaluate how dependent we ourselves are upon the approval of others. If it happens that we rely heavily upon others for our self-esteem, we will be more sensitive to criticism than if we have a strong belief in our own worth. In other words, is our spouse truly being critical or are we being hypersensitive, tending to take things too personally? This is not easy to determine without an objective third party.

Don and Ann came to my office because they were having some communication problems. Just after Ann had put a plate of spaghetti in front of Don for dinner, he took one bite and told her he didn't care much for spaghetti. How should this statement be interpreted? Oversensitive people would be insulted and hurt by this statement. They would react as if they heard their mate say, "You can't even make a decent batch of spaghetti." Yet it is perfectly reasonable for a person to decide not to like spaghetti as much as some of the other available menu options. Although the timing of this statement may imply that this particular batch of spaghetti was the deciding factor, this is not necessarily the case. Even if it were true, it is appropriate for Don to state how he feels and what he would prefer in the future.

On the other hand, if we are certain that our mate is definitely being critical and insensitive, we must be firm but nondefensive in dealing with our mate. If we are defensive or critical in return, we will only fuel an argument that will drive us and our mate further apart. It would be better to say, "Don, I am sorry that my cooking doesn't please you. But I need you to tell me what you do want without putting me down for what I have tried to do for you. I get discouraged when I don't know what I can do differently to please you."

Notice that Ann is asking for what she wants while not putting Don down for his critical behavior. She may have to repeat this kind of statement many, many times before Don begins to take her seriously. At least Ann is treating herself with respect in the meantime.

I must warn you against something at this point. People often say they have tried dealing with their mate in ways as I have suggested above and "it doesn't work." Their spouse continues to be dependent, aloof, controlling, critical, or whatever.

It is important to recognize that we are all free entities and we cannot control how others will respond to us. If we could control our mate, it would render the relationship meaningless. The purpose for sharing our feelings with our mate is not to control him or her, but to give the other person the opportunity to know and understand our needs better. In this way they can decide how they will respond to us in the future.

Once our partner hears how we feel, he or she may—or may not—try to meet that need. That is not our decision or responsibility. Some people have a difficult time changing. Others need a lot of consistent but kind confrontation to help them. But telling our mate what we want in a kind and constructive manner may be the only catalyst for change.

THE PHYSICALLY ABUSIVE SPOUSE

Physical abuse can be inflicted by either a husband or wife, although most perpetrators are men. Perhaps the wife has failed to meet her husband's expectations in some way, or his employment is not going well, or maybe he has had a few drinks on the way home. When he gets home he starts complaining and putting down his wife. When she objects to his irrational behavior, he begins to get violent. Her reaction, whatever it is, enrages him and he hits her or possibly even rapes her. How do we sing a love song to someone who is abusing us?

People who are married to physically abusive spouses are often unaware that they deserve any better treatment. This may sound strange to anyone who has never been abused. But for some, it is easier to tolerate abuse than to risk leaving the familiar and face the unknown. A woman may feel financially trapped with nowhere to go for help.

As Christians, our ultimate purpose is to love and glorify God by receiving his love and expressing it to others. Hopefully God is glorified by our marriage as we treat one another with loving behavior. Yet not every marriage honors God. Even in Christian homes there have been abusive situations that do not glorify God by reflecting his love in marriage. We cannot control our mates' behavior, but we must assume responsibility for our own. If we enable our mate to abuse us, we are participating in that person's behavior, which is dishonoring to God.

Our love song to an abusive spouse must be one of courage, whereby we stand up for what we believe and force our mate to face the consequences of such irresponsible behavior. Many women think that God wants them to be submissive to their husband's abuse. They fail to recognize that submission is to be mutual and out of loving respect (see Colossians 3:18-19). One-sided submission only allows insecure husbands to act irresponsibly while contradicting the broader view of Scripture to love one another mutually with patience and kindness (see 1 Corinthians 13:4).

Love is not indulgent. It holds people accountable for their actions. This helps them to grow in greater self-respect. "Tough" loving teaches others how to love and therefore glorifies God.

Jenny is a beautiful, middle-aged woman with three children. She loves her husband and has no desire to leave him. Jack is terribly insecure in spite of his incredible professional accomplishments as a successful dentist. He accuses Jenny of being interested in other men and frequently beats her up at home. Being a member of a church doesn't seem to make any difference in Jack's life. How many black eyes should Jenny suffer before she puts an end to this irrational behavior? It is reasonable to suffer for something in which we believe, and Jenny believed in her love for Jack. But she was having difficulty believing in Jack's love for her.

What was the most loving thing for her to do? Was it really loving for her to indulge Jack in his emotional immaturity and irresponsibility? Was it really loving for her to enable him to continue his abusive and destructive behavior? Was this really honoring to God to allow this abuse to continue? I do not believe so. Professional or pastoral counseling could be helpful here. It is difficult for victims of abuse to be objective about God's will for them.

In a situation like this where God's intent for marriage has been frustrated,[1] I believe it is more honoring to God for Jenny to separate from Jack so that he will be forced to look at himself and develop self-control. Of course the goal would be for Jenny to forgive Jack and reconcile with him if he could demonstrate true repentance and self-control.

Consideration of the following questions may be useful for an abused person contemplating separation:

1. Does your spouse try to control you with threats?

2. Is your physical safety threatened?

3. Are your children being abused physically or emotionally?

4. Does your mate admit to having a problem?

5. Has your mate been willing to seek help?

6. Has your mate shown any ability to benefit from professional help?

7. Are you strong enough emotionally and spiritually to deal with your abusive mate?

8. Are you becoming depressed or dysfunctional?

9. Is your self-esteem improving or getting worse due to this relationship?

10. Are you staying in the relationship out of fear or out of loving commitment?

11. Have you told your mate that he or she is hurting you and/or the children and you need the abuse to stop?

Marital commitment seeks to sing an enduring love song. However, sometimes we must endure from a distance. There are certain situations that, after careful consideration, may best be resolved by separation as an act of love toward the abuser. Love confronts a problem and is not indulgent of irresponsibility. This includes verbal and emotional abuse as well as physical abuse.

THE ILL SPOUSE

Sometimes it is not possible for our spouse to meet our needs even if he or she wanted to do so. Illness limits one's ability to give. Besides physical limitations, the resulting discomfort can cause one to be irritable and difficult to be around for extended periods of time. People in this position may need to hear a marital love song more than ever as they seek to cope with their condition.

Although many people remain cranky and bitter about their plight, I am amazed at how well some people do adjust to their circumstances. They learn to integrate their illness into their lifestyle and find creative ways to adapt to their condition. They learn to sing their own love song of inspiration to the caregiving spouse simply by their positive attitude of acceptance.

It is probably easier for the healthy partner to adapt to these difficult situations when the ill spouse has a positive attitude. Nevertheless, it is a major adjustment for both. Both have many unmet needs. How then do we deal with these needs not being met?

We have already discussed the importance of asking for what we want. This is more difficult to do with an ill spouse because of possibly unchanging limitations. In this case we must learn to ask for something that is within his or her ability to provide. This serves not only to meet our own needs, but also to help our mate feel genuinely valued in the relationship. People with severe limitations must work hard to find meaning and purpose for their lives. We can help them by affirming what they are able to give us.

What can Keith ask from his quadriplegic wife, Mary, who relies on others for practically everything?

"Mary, I am nervous about my meeting with the committee today. I would appreciate your prayers."

"I am really discouraged, dear. I guess I really need your encouragement and support."

"I love your kisses. I hope you don't run out of them."

"What do you think about my situation at work? How would you handle it?"

Although the ways an ill spouse can give may be limited in scope, his or her contribution can still be significant.

COPING WITH UNMET NEEDS

Now we must deal with how to handle ourselves when our needs are truly not met. We feel that we are doing all of the giving and none of the receiving. We have asked for what we want but have never gotten what we desire from our mate. We feel deeply hurt, frustrated, angry, and depressed. Our desires are never satisfied, our tensions are not resolved, and our lives are not finding satisfaction or fulfillment. What are we to do?

First of all, we must accept our humanness and face our feelings of disappointment and despair. Those who make the best adjustment to these difficult situations are those of us who are honest with ourselves about our feelings and allow ourselves to release pain. Tears are God's way of enabling us to release the emotional tension created by our pain. Releasing pain can either be done privately or with a trusted friend of the same sex. I recommend being with someone of the same sex because your vulnerability with someone of the opposite sex can facilitate a dangerous bonding between you that will only complicate your life if it occurs. If you have no one of your own gender with whom to share your pain, you might ask yourself why that is the case and seek to improve your situation. Counseling with your pastor may be beneficial at this point, not only to help you establish needed friendships, but to have a supportive person in your life until you can cultivate the needed friendships.

I would never want to discourage anyone from getting the counseling they need. But I do feel constrained to warn any potential counselee who is vulnerable and in need of emotional support to pay attention to how your counselor relates to you if you are being seen individually by a counselor of the opposite sex. Most ministers and counselors are safe to be with, but they are also human and may be going through a lonely time themselves.

In order to avoid any breach of professional conduct, you should be aware of and watch for a few things. Does your counselor have a picture of his or her spouse in the office? Is he or she wearing a wedding ring? Is there a window in the office? Does your counselor reveal personal details about himself or herself, or is the time spent focused on your issues as it should be? Remember that self-disclosure creates intimacy. If your counselor is being personally revealing to you when he or she knows you are vulnerable, this could be a danger sign. A professional minister-counselor should be sensitive, kind, and objective in dealing with your concerns. They should not be open personally with an opposite sex client who is vulnerable. This could lead to physical intimacy which is always inappropriate in a counseling relationship.

Being open and vulnerable in the presence of another person is threatening to some of us and easy for others. Those of us who find it difficult seek to avoid our painful feelings whenever possible. Yet this removes us from a conscious connection with our own feelings which is so important to healthy functioning. Those of us who have not learned to face our own emotional pain often turn to drugs, alcohol, sex, food, or whatever we can find to temporarily comfort ourselves. This only leads us, however, into addictive behavior. We don't realize that the best resolution to emotional pain is to experience it as fully as possible, preferably in the context of loving support from a trusted friend, relative, pastor, or counselor.

The next step in coping with marital frustration is to develop a network of friends from whom we can receive much of the loving acceptance and open communication we may not be getting at home. These relationships may be enjoyed on many levels. When we are hurting over our marriage, we have someone with whom to talk. When we simply need social contact, our same-gender friends may appreciate our call. By accepting responsibility for our own personal needs, we will have more positive experiences and feelings to share with our mate when we are together. This should enable us to be less frustrated and less demanding of our husband or wife.

The third suggestion for coping with a difficult marriage is to practice the presence of God in our life. The Scriptures tell us that God will never leave us or forsake us (see Hebrews 13:5). We can find strength in our relationship with God (see Psalm 46:1) and we can cast our burdens upon him (see 1 Peter 5:7), finding strength (see Psalm 55:22). Nothing can separate us from his love (see Romans 8:38-9). Prayer and meditation can give us strength when we need it the most.

We sing a love song of commitment by asking for what we want while also accepting the personal limitations of our mate's response to us. Accepting people for who they are without resentment is more likely when we accept responsibility for our own pain and reach out to God and our church community for alternative resources that can nurture us in positive, wholesome ways. We may not always sing on key, but these special efforts enable us to sing and to keep singing an enduring love song to our mate.

Finally, let's round out our discussion of marital commitment by considering the role played by our often-subconscious beliefs and expectations. We need to learn more about ourselves, especially if we want to head off trouble before it cripples our marriage.

CHAPTER TEN

The Believing
Love Song

Gary and Linda believed they had a great marriage. They were two attractive people, young, energetic, as close to fulfilling their dream as anyone could hope to be. Gary was moving ahead professionally, they were ready to start a family, and they had a lot of friends from church whom they enjoyed regularly. As a couple, they enjoyed each other very much and always seemed to know how to get their needs met. In fact they had always been "winners." They were both used to getting their own way ever since childhood.

Yet with all of this going for them, there was one major problem in their relationship that neither of them could see. Because they had always known how to get what they wanted in life, they never learned to deal with tragedy and pain. As long as everything was going along fine, they were safe. Along with many other couples, however, Gary and Linda did not build their marriage on a belief system solid enough to sustain them through difficult times. They were married for three wonderful years before things started to change.

Linda was diagnosed with multiple sclerosis. She had no choice but to accept and deal with her illness. Gary, however, divorced her within the year. His expectation of an ideal life had been tampered with. He resented it. He couldn't face the fact that Linda would have to slow down and not be as available for him as she had been in the past. He had big plans for "getting ahead" and Linda's condition would have interfered. He would have needed to make some adjustments in his lifestyle and help out more with what used to be all her responsibilities. Linda could no longer meet Gary's expectations.

What Gary believed about his marriage was not sufficient to keep him committed to it.

The strength of our marital commitment depends upon what it is that we believe about marriage. We cannot commit ourselves to something in which we do not believe. Therefore it is imperative that we have positive beliefs about our marriage in order to maximize its longevity. What we believe about marriage affects the strength of our marital commitment.

Weak marriages are built upon unrealistic expectations. I encounter these expectations regularly in my counseling practice. I want to list some of the more frequent ones because I believe they are important to recognize, inasmuch as they undermine marital commitment. Although my clients reveal their expectations in many cryptic ways, the uncoded version is usually something like what you are about to read.

MISCONCEPTIONS ABOUT MARRIAGE

1. "My mate will always be responsive to my needs." We would all like to have a mate who is responsive to our needs. However, it is unlikely that we shall ever experience being married to someone who meets *all* of our needs *all* of the time. It is not really possible for one person to be all things to another. If it were possible we would become very spoiled and so dependent that it would be a very difficult adjustment to make if we were ever to lose such a spouse. Furthermore, in order to truly appreciate what our mate does give us, we occasionally need to experience unmet needs.

Expecting our mate to always meet our needs undermines our commitment to marriage when it happens that our mate doesn't meet our expectations.

2. "If I am willing to give, so will my mate." At best this notion recognizes that giving in marriage is important. At worst, this person may get upset and feel unloved if the other one does not reciprocate in the time and manner that he or she would like.

"Giving to get" is not giving at all. The problem with this belief is that giving seems conditional upon getting something back. A true gift demands nothing in return. Marriage is for giving what we are able to give and for receiving whatever there is to receive. Giving to our mate is an opportunity to sing our love song.

It is unrealistic to expect our mate to echo our love song every time we sing it. Love does not require an echo. Love seeks no guarantees. Love seeks the ultimate good for the beloved. Of course we can expect to be loved, but not necessarily in return for what we have specifically given. We expect to be loved because our mate has demonstrated in the past that he or she does in fact love us. Love is not a reward. It is not something for which we bargain or perform. It is merely received when offered.

Many of us feel from time to time that we are doing all of the giving. We may be. And at the risk of sounding like a broken record, let me say once again: we *can* ask for what we want.

However, our responsibility is not to keep score, but to nurture ourselves in a variety of constructive ways in order to give without resenting it or demanding something back. Love does not give on a conditional basis. Marital commitment based upon getting back in equal portions is a fragile commitment.

3. "Our love will enable us to feel the same about everything." If two people (especially a male and a female) ever feel the same about everything, then one of them is asleep! They may have a high level of agreement, but to agree on everything suggests that somebody is being very passive. Passivity may make the dominant person feel in charge, but such dominance is preventing the passive individual from becoming a complete person. It is unfortunate that so many people have been reared, even in Christian homes, to think that to love and serve others means to be a "nothing" or a "nobody" without any personal opinions or desires.

Christian maturity involves having a strong sense of who we are, with definite opinions, strong convictions, and clear needs, all of which we bring into subjection to Christ. Becoming a disciple of Jesus is not possible if we do not have a sense of our *self*, a self that can choose to serve him.

The passive person is taking the easy way out. By being a "nothing," there is no risk in giving oneself away. The problem is that society gets exactly that too... nothing. Christian maturity involves becoming a full self, subservient to Christ and submitting to each other in love.

The need to agree on everything is an unsound basis for a marital commitment. Disagreement helps keep us alert as we reevaluate our position on matters of mutual concern. The problem comes when one or both has to be seen as right because we are too insecure to risk being seen as wrong. However, love does not have to be right, for love is honest and just and seeks only the truth.

If you and your mate do feel the same about everything, you might consider whether or not one of you does all the thinking for both of you.

4. "I can change my spouse over time." Some people marry thinking that those little obnoxious "quirks" of their mate will go away over time with the "right kind of supervision." Maybe they will and maybe they won't.

We often want our mate to change so we will be comfortable. It is always easier to expect the other to change than for us to take responsibility for dealing with our own feelings about things that our spouse does.

If, for example, you don't like the fact that your wife leaves all the lights on in the house even when they are not needed, you have three options: (1) Turn them out yourself. (2) Ask her to turn them out when not using them. (3) Let the lights burn until you figure out what really bugs you about it. Is it really that costly? Were your parents stingy with lighting? Are you taking it personally by feeling that she is doing it just to bug you? Or is it possible that it just isn't important to her? When you realize that you are simply two different people with two different backgrounds, it may become easier to accept her way, once you have shared your feelings with her.

Is wanting to change our mate a sound basis for commitment to our marriage? What happens to our marital commitment if there is no change?

Christian marriage is an arrangement where two people can both enjoy being loved and accepted for who they are without having to change to be acceptable, although we are free to change. We cannot control what our spouse does. We can, however, take responsibility for our own behavior and act accepting of our mate as a person.

5. "My mate should know what I want without my having to ask." I frequently encounter couples in my counseling practice who find it very difficult to ask for what they want. Some people aren't sure what they want in the first place. They just rely on their mate to make them happy.

Others know what they want but absolutely refuse to reveal it. If you can't figure out what they want, you just don't love them enough, or so it would seem. Many of us are very sensitive and easily hurt when we perceive ourselves being rejected. To ask for something that might not be granted would be very threatening. So we don't ask for something that we are afraid we might not get.

When we were infants, Mom had a way of knowing what we needed even though we were too young to speak. Some of us even had very attentive and responsive parents as we grew older. If this was overdone, however, we learned to expect that same treatment from other people, especially our spouses.

This leads us into unrealistic expectations of our mate.

It is a big shock to realize that our mate does not have the same notion that we do about asking for what is wanted. This is an important issue to clear up between you since unfulfilled expectations can undermine marital commitment.

6. "If I must ask for what I want, I should get it." Some of us want the security of knowing that we will get what we want, without refusal, rejection, or humiliation. Of course, this expectation is not upon what committed marriages are built.

As we have noted in other contexts, love expresses itself regardless of what comes back. Love does not seek the security of guarantees, because love's priority is that it be expressed, not that it be accepted.

Of course we all want to be accepted. However, as soon as we attach the conditional strings of security to our love, we undermine our love. For love has no strings attached, requires no security, and is not afraid. Perfect love casts out fear (1 John 4:18). God has not given us the spirit of fear, but of love, power, and a sound mind (see 2 Timothy 1:7).

7. "We shouldn't have to discuss unpleasant things." Nobody would be so naive as to actually say this, yet many of us show that we believe it by avoiding certain issues.

Some of us don't like to face up to problems because we feel inadequate in trying to solve them. Some husbands, for example, would rather have their wives handle the child's medical emergency without discussing it. Or a wife might not want to hear about how her husband could lose his job. She just wants him to handle it. Obviously ignoring such problems doesn't make them go away.

But marriage is a partnership where two people share in the joys and the burdens of life together. Marital devotion based upon the avoidance of uncomfortable conversation does not provide a strong base for marital commitment. When problems can no longer be avoided, we may avoid the marriage.

8. "If my spouse loves me, he or she will do what I want." This is the most unrealistic belief of all. The person who expects this is saying that whatever we value is what our spouse should do for us. We should always remember that love cannot be controlled. It can only be received. We cannot tell our mate how to love us. We must learn to listen for our mate's own love song just as he or she must learn to listen for our love song.

Although we can let our mate know what our favorite songs are, we are not acting in love if we demand they perform to our satisfaction. One of our love songs to our mate is to accept the love song he or she sings to us.

Marital commitment based upon the other's performance is dangerous. What happens when the other does not meet our expectations? Do we blame and criticize our mate for not being what we think he or she should be? Or do we give our spouse the same level of acceptance that we ourselves so desire from our beloved?

The problem with these unrealistic expectations in marriage is that they are self-centered needs, dependent upon our partner for satisfaction. If we are committed to marriage because of these expectations, what happens when these expectations are not met? People are leaving relationships right and left because they aren't getting what they have wanted. When their needs are not getting met, they can no longer see the value of being married. If the extent of our belief about our marriage is limited to the expectation of satisfying our personal needs, then our relationship is on thin ice.

People who hold to these expectations usually do not realize that they are doing so. They act them out without even thinking about it. So I challenge you to ask your mate if he or she thinks *you* have any of these expectations.

In his book, *Habits of the Heart*, Robert Bellah speaks at length about the individualistic trend in our society.[1] We have become a nation of people who want what we want when we want it. We are used to getting our way and getting it quickly. "Fast food" and "fast relationships" are characteristic of our times. The consequences of this "quick fix" mentality are that we are so used to getting what we want that we don't know how to handle frustration, disappointment, and emotional pain. We are too quick to assume that there can be no real value or benefit in our momentary suffering. We are so used to running from discomfort that people think we are crazy if we speak of what we have learned from our painful experiences. Sadly some of us will never find the joy behind our suffering because we aren't willing to face it long enough to discover what it willteach us about ourselves. If we have some sense of the meaning and purpose of our pain, we will be much stronger in our response to it.

Joy can be found in suffering with a purpose. We can lovingly accept our mate's inability to meet certain of our needs. We can find joy in this because God's love in us is greater than our fear, frustration, and unresolved tensions.

Marital commitment is only as strong as a husband and wife's combined convictions about their marriage. Both parties must believe in something about their relationship that is more stable than personal-need satisfaction. If our marital commitment is based solely upon getting specific forms of love, comfort, and attention from our mate, then we have little motivation to sustain our marriage when those ideals are not available to us.

It is my conviction that our marital commitment can only be as strong as our beliefs about our marriage. When I ask people what they believe about their marriage, they have a difficult time answering the question. I am going to share with you some beliefs that I consider to be basic and important for every Christian couple. Subscribing to these beliefs will lead us toward more realistic expectations in our marriage and strengthen our own marital commitment.

CHRISTIAN BELIEFS ABOUT MARRIAGE

1. Marital commitment is a promise to devote ourselves to the preservation of our marriage regardless of changing feelings or circumstances. If we believe that the meaning of our marriage embraces more than the fulfillment of our own personal needs, then our marital commitment will rest upon a strong foundation when our own personal needs are not fully being met.

2. The strongest motivation for marital commitment lies in the belief that "it is more blessed to give than to receive" (Acts 20:35). This is not to imply that receiving is not important, for if nobody received, giving would have no meaning. We need to balance giving with receiving. Yet choosing to give to others is ultimately more joyous than receiving for ourselves. Love is the happiest when it is giving because giving is the nature of love. As obedient children of God we are happiest fulfilling our created purpose of giving love.

3. God's greatest commandment to us is to love him and others as ourselves (see Matthew 22:37-9). Our love for God is demonstrated by our obedience to him in loving our mate and others. According to the Bible, the way we treat our mate and other people is the way we are treating God (see Matthew 25:40). Love is the fulfillment of God's law (see Romans 13:8).

4. Loving our mate and others in obedience to God is actually an act of worship toward God. Matthew 25:40 quotes Jesus as saying, "Whatever you did for one of the least of these brothers of mine, you did for me."

Furthermore, Romans 12:1 tells us that it is a spiritual act of worship to offer our bodies as living sacrifices, holy and pleasing to God. Loving is often sacrificial. It often means putting our mate's needs ahead of our own.

5. Loving each other is a testimony to the world of God's love. "The fruit of the Spirit" includes love (Gal 5:22). We are told in John 13:35, "By this all men will know that you are my disciples, if you love one another."

We are told in 1 Corinthians 13:1 that without love, our lives are just a lot of noise. Real love, on the other hand, tells the world that God is alive and well in those of us who demonstrate his love in our lives. We can strengthen our marital commitment by realizing that marriage is an opportunity to present God's love to the world.

6. God wants to love us through each other. One of the ways God demonstrates his love toward us is through our mate. God wants to love us through our mate and he wants to love our mate through us. We are told in 1 John 3:24 that "those who obey his commands live in him, and he in them."

Believing that God wants to love us through each other keeps us aware of the importance of marital commitment in God's ultimate purpose for us.

7. Loving gives our lives significance. We all want to feel important. We all want to be recognized and treated as if our life matters to somebody. We want credit for what we do. We want to be loved and wanted by others. We desire to feel accepted (even though we don't always accept others). Acceptance and recognition seem to be great needs in our society.

Our greatest significance comes not from being loved, but in giving love. People need our love. This means that the most important people in the world are those who give love to others. If we want to feel important to our mate, we need to love our mate, purposefully. However, it is not our mate's validating response that we must have to feel important, but rather our belief that God's love in us has a powerful and positive effect on others. Our life is significant in passing God's love on to our mate regardless of the response we receive.

I have known many clients who have held themselves back from giving love because of their low self-esteem. They couldn't believe that their love was significant enough to impact their spouse's life in any meaningful way. By not reaching out, they deprived their mate of love, in the process undermining their own significance as one who loves. We need to act in faith and not allow our negative feelings to keep us from opportunities for loving.

The road to positive self-esteem is a long and difficult one for those who have been criticized or rejected in their younger years. However, my experience has taught me that the key to recovery is choosing to believe in God's love for us rather than believing our negatively trained emotions. This may require counseling, support, and a relationship where we can experience acceptance of our thoughts and feelings while still being accountable for our behavior. This help can come through a counselor, friend, and our relationship with God. Praying regularly is essential to keep us in touch with God's loving acceptance.

8. Together, our lives are blessed differently than if we are apart because we can do things together that we cannot do

alone. We can work together as servants of God in ministry to other couples. We can support each other in our mate's individual ministry. We can bring the best out in each other and encourage our mate to reach his or her full potential to glorify God. Believing this will strengthen our marital commitment.

9. Marriage is a gift from God. Our mate is a gift from God. Obviously, everyone doesn't believe this. Some feel their marriage was a mistake.

However, changing our self-image from "victim" to "lover" and viewing our mate as an opportunity for us to participate in God's expression of love is the kind of belief and perspective that strengthens our marital commitment.

10. For our spouse to benefit from it, love must be expressed in behavior. In the New Testament, beliefs and actions are considered synonymous. It is assumed that we will act upon what we believe. First John 3:18 tells us not to "love with words or tongue but with *actions* and in truth."

Acting on the belief that love is a behavior will strengthen our marital commitment because such behavior will generate loving feelings. When our belief in love is acted upon, loving feelings are the eventual result.

At the same time, we are warned in Romans 12:9 that love must be sincere. Acting loving even if we do not feel loving at the moment is sincere as long as we believe it is the right thing to do. As Christians we are commanded to do it. It is our *belief* that must be sincere, not our feeling. We are to love even our enemies, not because we feel like it, but because we believe it is right to obey Christ who gave us the command.

11. Our marital commitment can be strengthened by believing that true love is unconditional. God does not accept us according to our level of performance or how we look. First

Samuel 16:7 tells us, "The Lord does not look at the things man looks at. Man looks at the outward appearance, but the Lord looks at the heart."

God loves us just for *being,* and he wants us to love our mate from the same perspective. How old our mate is or how young he or she looks is irrelevant to God and should be to us as well. Our love must not depend upon how we are treated or how well our mate satisfies us. To love unconditionally means to act loving to our mate regardless of the immediate circumstances. Even if our mate is hurting our feelings, we are not to retaliate, although we may indicate that we experience the actions as hurtful.

Although the guiding principle must always be unconditional love, it is important to understand that love is not indulgent or always "nice" to get our mate's approval. There are occasions where love must be tough.[2]

We are told in 1 Corinthians 16:14 to "do everything in love." In Matthew 5:44, Jesus tells us to love our enemies and pray for those who persecute us. Love is always the guideline for living. Even if our mate is the "enemy" at the moment, we are to love him or her with our attitude and our actions.

Believing in unconditional love is the first step toward living it. Our marital commitment is strengthened by belief in the unconditional nature of love.

12. The ability to love our mate and others comes from a relationship with God. If we believe that we have a close relationship with God, we will seek to honor him through loving our mate. It is difficult to love God and not love our mate.

The Bible tells us that God is love (see 1 John 4:16). God desires to live in us and love our mate through us. When we love each other, God's love is made complete in us (see 1 John 4:12).

Our relationship with God, however, is interrupted by our

human tendency to act and live independent of God (see Romans 3:23). This alienates us from the very Source of love. As we seek to live our lives apart from God, our capacity to love our mate is undermined. Independence from God leads us to spiritual death (see Romans 6:23) and marital ruin.

God knew we would need more than this conviction in order to live lives of love. Because he knew that we could not have life independent from his love, he reached out to touch our hearts with it. Christ gave up his life for us that all who believe in him will have their relationship with God restored (see John 3:16). Jesus Christ is the bridge back to God (see 1 Timothy 2:5; John 14:6) as well as the bridge back to our mate and to other broken relationships. We love God because he first loved us (see 1 John 4:19). Christ's love then compels us to love our mate with a committed love. Since Christ died in our place we should no longer live for ourselves, but for Christ (see 2 Corinthians 5:14-15).

What we believe about marriage, God, and our own purpose in life holds the key to marital commitment. If we truly believe the tenets above, they will strengthen our ability to go the distance in our marriage. Believing in these principles gives our marriage direction, purpose, endurance, and stability to rise above the stress and strain of relational problems.

Believing that marriage is more about giving than getting redefines our personal expectations. When our dreams are not fulfilled, we need not view our marriage as a mistake.

Commitment is the stabilizing force that steadies our relationship when troubles threaten to swamp our marriage. When the winds of passion fail to fill the sail of our loveboat, commitment is the auxiliary engine that keeps us from drifting off course. In fact commitment pushes us toward fresh new currents of wind, restoring our passion and motivating us toward intimate loving.

Being committed to our marriage by treating our mate with love is an opportunity for us to fulfill our created purpose and be joyfully connected to God's eternal love song.

Let us briefly consider how the primary love songs of passion, intimacy, and commitment harmonize together.

How to Sing
a Love Song

We have been looking at three areas vital to any loving relationship. Furthermore, we have sought to explore these areas of passion, intimacy, and commitment from a Christian perspective to help us enrich our own marriage.

We have learned that marital passion is a strong desire to be close to our mate. Passion stirs us into loving action thereby affirming both the lover and the beloved. Passion brings energy for loving to a relationship because it is a mixture of desire and hope for loving and being loved.

Without marital passion, a relationship becomes passive, routine, and boring. Many passionless marriages stay together out of commitment, but a relationship without passion is like a sailboat without a breeze.

Passion alone, however, could never sustain a relationship. For passion thrives on the hope of fulfillment. Passion is unstable when it sees no hope of achieving intimacy with one's beloved.

Passion is brought to its fulfillment by marital intimacy, mutual familiarity with our mate. Intimacy is not a goal that is achieved once and forever. Intimacy can only survive in rhythmic alternation with passion. If we become terminally engrossed in our achievement of intimacy, we become dependent and fail to participate in keeping the relationship awake and alive. On the other hand, if we have passion without intimacy our fire will eventually burn out without the fuel of fulfillment. The life of a loving relationship throbs with the heartbeat of passion and intimacy.

Intimacy is also important because it reveals us to each other so that we can know how to love each other. We can only love someone to the extent that we know them. Intimacy provides us with details of each other's personal thoughts and feelings, giving us a means by which we can involve ourselves in a loving and supportive way with one another. The less intimate a relationship is, the less love can be shared.

Marital commitment is a promise to persist at maintaining the relationship. Commitment is strongest when based upon clear positive beliefs about love, marriage, and God. Strong beliefs can override impulsive actions or feelings of discontent and discouragement. When we know what we believe we have direction and purpose. When our purpose in life is to fulfill that for which we believe we were created—namely, to love—then we know that we have a powerful auxiliary engine in our love boat that can keep us on course when the winds of passion fail to fill our sails.

Commitment keeps the heartbeat of passion and intimacy going. A marriage built on commitment alone would be mechanical and cold. It might be admired for its stability, but without the excitement and warmth of passion and intimacy, committed love is not complete. We want all the right elements in our love songs.

The power to love our mate with passion, intimacy, and commitment comes from having a relationship with God. The God of the Universe, who created the earth and all of us who inhabit it, is the best love-song Composer of all. Far from being an inaccessible Supreme Being, he is love itself. With all love, he sent his Son, Jesus Christ, to bridge the gap between our humanness and his holiness. Now we can love, because he first loved us (1 Jn 4:19).

A man and a woman who become husband and wife can partake of his heavenly love; with God's help, they can sing their love songs on key.

We all know that a marriage can be a joy or a nightmare. Discord and disharmony enter in automatically if we don't follow God's precepts. Unless we know and follow him, our best efforts are quickly exhausted. If we cooperate with him, our individual lives and our marriages can become an unending symphony of joyful praise.

This joyful, God-inspired marriage symphony is one that includes these three essential themes: passion, intimacy, and commitment.

Notes

SIX
The Revealing Love Song

1. Carol Tavris, *Anger: The Misunderstood Emotion* (New York: Simon and Schuster, 1982).

EIGHT
The Biblical Love Song

1. Kenneth Bailey, "New Testament Themes" videotape (Wichita, Kan.: Harvest Communications) Videotape 6, Part II.
2. Keith Korstjens, *Not a Sometimes Love* (Waco, Tex.: Word, 1983).
3. Alan Richardson, ed., *A Theological Wordbook of the Bible* (New York: Macmillan, 1950).
4. George Arthur Buttrick, ed., *Interpreter's Dictionary of the Bible* (Nashville, Tenn.: Abingdon, 1962).
5. Bailey, videotape.
6. James C. Dobson, *Love Must Be Tough* (Waco, Tex.: Word, 1983).

NINE
The Enduring Love Song

1. Diogenes Allen, *Love* (Cambridge: Cowley, 1987), 110.

TEN
The Believing Love Song

1. Robert N. Bellah, *Habits of the Heart* (New York: Harper & Row, 1985).
2. Dobson, *Love Must Be Tough.*

Bibliography

Allen, Diogenes. *Love*. Cambridge: Cowley, 1987.

Alsdurf, Jim, and Phyllis Alsdurf. *Battered Into Submission*. Minnetonka: InterVarsity, 1984.

Bellah, Robert N., Richard Madsen, William M. Sullivan, Ann Swidler, and Steven M. Tipton. *Habits of the Heart*. New York: Harper & Row, 1985.

Bailey, Kenneth. "New Testament Theme," videotape 6 on 1 Corinthians 13, Part II. Wichita: Harvest Communications.

Barker, Kenneth, ed. *The New International Version Study Bible*. Grand Rapids: Zondervan, 1985.

Bruner, Frederick Dale. *The Christbook*. Waco: Word, 1987.

Buttrick, George Arthur, ed. *Interpreter's Dictionary of the Bible*. Nashville: Abingdon, 1962.

Diehm, William J. *Staying in Love*. Minneapolis: Augsburg, 1986.

Dobson, James C. *Love Must Be Tough*. Waco: Word, 1983.

Garland, Diana S. Richmond, and David E. Garland. *Beyond Companionship: Christians in Marriage*. Philadelphia: Westminster, 1986.

Korstjens, Keith. *Not a Sometimes Love*. Waco: Word, 1983.

Richardson, Alan, ed. *A Theological Wordbook of the Bible.* New York: Macmillan, 1950.

Sternberg, Robert J. *The Triangle of Love.* New York: Basic Books, 1988.

Tavris, Carol. *Anger: The Misunderstood Emotion.* New York: Simon & Schuster, 1982.